Learning About . . .

The Holocaust

Learning About . . .

The Holocaust

Literature and Other Resources
for Young People

■   ■   ■

Elaine C. Stephens, Jean E. Brown, Janet E. Rubin

Library Professional Publications—1995

First published 1995 as a Library Professional Publication,
an imprint of The Shoe String Press, Inc.,
North Haven, Connecticut 06473.

Stephens, Elaine C.
  Learning about the Holocaust . . . literature and other resources
for young people / Elaine C. Stephens, Jean E. Brown, Janet E. Rubin.
     p.   cm.
ISBN 0–208–02398–4 (cloth : alk. paper).
ISBN 0–208–02408–5, (paper : alk. paper)
  1. Holocaust, Jewish (1939–1945)—Juvenile literature—Bibliography.
2. Holocaust, Jewish (1939–1945)—Juvenile literature. 3. Holocaust, Jewish
(1939–1945)—Study and teaching. I. Brown, Jean E. II. Rubin, Janet.
III. Title. Z6374.H6S74   1995
[D804.3]
940.53′18—dc20   95-31545
                                                          CIP
                                                          AC

The paper in this publication meets the minimum requirements
of American National Standard for Information Sciences—
Permanence of Paper for Printed Library Materials.
ANSI Z39.48–1984. ⊗

Printed in the United States of America

For my new grandson, Griffin Scott Graham, with the sincere desire that his generation learns the lessons of the Holocaust.—Elaine C. Stephens

In loving memory of my mother, Iza R. Brown, who, by her daily example, taught me the meaning of tolerance, kindness, and respect.—Jean E. Brown

To the Levin family, and especially to Becky Schwartz, for the faith and love they have always shared.—Janet E. Rubin

Contents

Acknowledgments

Many people provided us with encouragement and support as we researched and wrote this book. With gratitude and affection, we acknowledge Nadine Burke, Associate Professor of English, Delta College. She loaned us materials, critiqued the manuscript, and encouraged us throughout the entire process. To Kristy L. Brosius, Resource Center Coordinator, United States Holocaust Memorial Museum, who provided us with valuable information and advice, we also express our appreciation.

This book reflects the vision and knowledge of our editor, Diantha Thorpe. We thank her for her belief in the importance of this book, her steady guidance during its development, and her incredible attention to detail.

Family members supported us with their interest and patience. For this, we thank Wes Stephens, Melinda Stephens Graham, Tom Graham, Vesta Brown Mitchell, Jessica Brown, and Shirley Rubin Friedland.

Among others to whom we express our appreciation are Flora B. Atkin, Kathy Fehrman, Sharon Gorrell, Judy Kerman, Jan Lyddon, David E. Nelson, Ken Solway, Dee Storey, and Saun Strobel.

And finally, we express our appreciation to the many fine teachers and librarians we have known and worked with throughout the years. They remain the impetus and inspiration for our endeavors.

Introduction

The first to perish were the children . . . from these a new
dawn might have risen.

Yitzhak Katzenelson
Wall of Remembrance,
U. S. Holocaust Memorial Museum

We have written this resource book for teachers, librarians, youth
leaders, counselors, parents, and other adults who work with
young people in a variety of educational, cultural, and religious
settings. It will assist adults in selecting and using literature and
other materials about the Holocaust and its aftermath with today's
young people, kindergarten through high school. Suggestions and
activities are provided to help young people become actively involved in this literature and to give them help and guidance as they
learn.

Holocaust literature is a rapidly expanding field. We reviewed close
to 300 titles to select the ones we recommend in this resource guide.
Our selection criteria included literary quality, historical authentic-
ity, effectiveness in fostering an intellectual and emotional connection with the subject, and appropriateness for each age group.

While no guide can be completely comprehensive, it is our hope that the titles and authors recommended in this book will serve as a useful starting point for gaining an understanding of what happened, and why, in the Holocaust.

How to Use This Book

In chapter 1, we present an historical overview of the Holocaust and a rationale for using its literature with young people. Chapters 2 through 6 provide annotated plot summaries and listings of chosen literary works written for young people, as well as suggestions for using these works. Each chapter is organized thematically by genre. The titles include informational books, photo essays, picture books, biographies, personal narratives, poems, historical fiction, plays, and realistic fiction. Within each chapter, the works are organized according to grade level designations. Chapter 7 provides information on additional resources for learning about the Holocaust, including other media, curriculum materials, and organizations.

While each chapter has a special focus, it is not necessary to go through the book, chapter by chapter, in sequential order. Each chapter stands by itself and can be used in any order as it meets the needs of the readers. While some readers may want to focus exclusively on the works in one chapter, others may want to use information from several chapters in combination, such as an informational selection from chapter 2 along with a personal narrative from chapter 3 and an appropriate play from chapter 5 or an accompanying video/film from chapter 7.

Chapters 2 through 6 give extensive information on a group of representative titles, followed by more abbreviated annotations on additional works of the same type that can also be used with youthful readers. Each chapter begins with a brief introduction to the type of literature in it and its value in helping young people learn about the Holocaust. Next, the feature "Prior to Reading: Think About . . ." has questions for young people to consider before they begin reading the literature recommended in the chapter. This is followed by "Focus," which offers specific entries organized by grade level. "Focus" is structured as follows:

1. Quotes from the work that can be used to interest young people in reading the work or to promote post-reading discussion

2. Bibliographic citation including suggested grade designations:
   - AL — All School Levels
   - P — Primary School Level (grades K-2)
   - E — Elementary School Level (grades 3–5/6)
   - JM — Junior High/Middle School Level
   - S — Secondary School Level

3. A brief description of the work entitled "At a Glance," which includes a recommendation for the appropriate grade levels

4. A summary of the work

5. Teaching considerations consisting of suggestions for the particular work and recommendations for related works

Next are abbreviated entries on additional titles, "Further Reading for All Levels," consisting of the bibliographic citation, a brief description, and a recommendation. All of these entries will help adults to guide young people in their selection of literature appropriate for their ages and level of understanding. Following the entries, we provide "Literature Involvement: Suggestions and Issues for Responding and Thinking" based on the works in the chapter. These ideas are designed to heighten connections with the literature and to help youthful readers grapple with and understand the complexities and horrors of the Holocaust.

A word of caution regarding grade designations is in order. Grade designations should never be strictly adhered to when matching a particular work with a specific young person. A common error committed by adults when selecting books on complex and sensitive subjects such as the Holocaust is to provide students with materials that appear to be at their reading level, but actually require a higher level of intellectual sophistication and emotional maturity to truly grasp. We recommend, therefore, that students be given less complex material to begin with and then as they acquire a conceptual base of understanding and demonstrate an emotional readiness, be gradually introduced to more difficult material.

Additionally, there is a wide variation among students within any grade or age level. More important than the grade designation per se is the individual's background knowledge, interest, and maturity. For example, some elementary school students will be comfortable reading books designated both for elementary and junior high/middle school students; others will find books designated for primary school children to be more appropriate. Some secondary students whose background knowledge is limited or who are reluctant readers will benefit more from books designed for junior high/middle school students. Increasingly, picture books, which used to be written exclusively for young children, are appropriate for readers of all ages, especially when addressing complex and sensitive subjects. Plays, likewise, provide important variety and appeal for readers. Perhaps the best approach is to provide a wide range of materials and help students to select those that make the best match. Another approach that is effective with all grade levels is to read aloud excerpts or, in some cases, entire selections. Reading aloud provides students with a common experience and promotes thinking and discussion.

We use the following system to recommend grade levels for each title. The first letter following the bibliographic citation indicates the most appropriate grade level. If the book is used as a representative title, this letter also indicates where to find information about the book in the chapter. The next letters indicate the other grade levels that could be appropriate. Here are three examples:

Adler, David A. Illustrated by Karen Ritz. *A Picture Book of Anne Frank*. Holiday House, 1993. 29 pages. (P, E)

The P indicates that this book is appropriate for young children. It could be read aloud to primary school children, grades K–2. It also is appropriate for elementary school students, grades 3–5/6. Although the citation will be listed in several places in the chapter, a summary of its contents will be located under the heading, Primary School Level.

Matas, Carol. *Daniel's Story*. Scholastic/United States Holocaust Memorial Museum, 1993. 136 pages. (JM, E, S)

This book has wide appeal. While it is probably most appropriate for junior high/middle school students, it could be read aloud to elementary school children or read independently by some; the action and high interest also make it appealing to some secondary school students. Although the citation will be listed in several places in the chapter, a summary of its contents will be located under the heading, Junior High/Middle School Level.

Berenbaum, Michael. Arnold Kramer, photography editor. *The World Must Know. The History of the Holocaust as Told in the United States Holocaust Memorial Museum*. Little, Brown, 1993. 240 pages. (S, JM)

The S indicates that this book is most appropriate for secondary school students; it also is appropriate for some junior high/middle students. Although the citation will be listed in several places in the chapter, a summary of its contents will be located under the heading, Secondary School Level.

I

Background

We Must Remember

Soon there will be no one left alive who personally lived
through the Holocaust. So, it becomes even more
important to remember those terrible years and how they
began, and to remember how cruelty, hatred and
discrimination led to violence, death and destruction.

Norman Finkelstein, *Remember Not to Forget:*
A Memory of the Holocaust

When we speak of the Holocaust, we utter the unspeakable; when
we think of the Holocaust, we acknowledge the unimaginable; yet
this is a chapter of our history that must be told so people of conscience will never let the horror happen again. The Holocaust is
more than the story of the six million Jews who perished in the
death camps; it is more than the story of the destruction of Gypsies,
homosexuals, and political prisoners. It is the story of brutality and
savagery. It is the story of a society gone mad where maniacal horror reigns and daily life is a balancing act between fear and hope
that the nightmare will end. It is the story of the world's inability
to comprehend the magnitude of crimes against humanity. The Holocaust is also the story of those who survived and those who risked
everything to help others to escape the inevitability of the camps.

While the Holocaust is the darkest chapter of our history, it contains some of the brightest pages. On these pages are written the triumph of the human spirit in acts of courage and decency that saved numerous lives. But these acts translate into more than individual lives being saved: they are acts that reaffirm basic human belief in the dignity of the human spirit and its ability to transcend even the basest acts of those who seek to control and destroy. Among the painful and tragic lessons of the Holocaust there is also a vital message of courage from those who perished and a vibrant message of hope from those who survived and those who helped them. Those who experienced the Holocaust have stories to tell; stories that will inspire, horrify, and enlighten young readers. This book is written to honor not only those who perished during the Holocaust, but also the survivors and their supporters. Through their acts of bravery and courage they have given the world cause to celebrate. We celebrate their lives and courage by promising to keep the message alive in the hope that this type of carnage will never again happen.

No chapter in modern history has resulted in as resounding infamy as the systematic attempts of Adolf Hitler and the Nazis to annihilate European Jews and others to establish his Aryan "Master Race." How could this happen? In chapter 6 we examine literature that illustrates ongoing examples of bigotry and discrimination as well as that which reflects upon past discrimination. While certainly the long history of Jewish persecution contributed to the events of the Holocaust, we must also examine more immediate causes.

Post-World War I Germany was demoralized by defeat. This feeling was intensified by economic conditions as the worldwide depression affected Germany. The country was in need of direction and leadership. This void was filled by a failed artist and house painter from Austria named Adolf Hitler. Hitler had wandered aimlessly as a young man until he served in the German Army in World War I. He served with distinction as a dispatch runner and was awarded the Iron Cross, First Class. He was a corporal when his military career was ended by mustard gas, which left him temporarily blind. During his blindness he became obsessed with the delusion that he was destined to be an Aryan hero who would lead Germany. When his sight returned, he became committed to saving Germany. He joined with other veterans and became a member of the German Worker's party in 1919, the forerunner to the National Socialist, or Nazi, party.

Hitler was a charismatic orator who became the leader of the party by 1921. He and his supporters attracted numbers of young men who were unemployed. Hitler created a special corps of these men with allegiance only to him and dressed them in brown-shirted uniforms. He created the trappings of organization, the Nazi flag with its black swastika, the Nazi salute of the arm raised to the chant of *"Sieg Heil,"* ("Hail to Victory") or *"Heil Hitler,"* and the brown shirts of his storm troopers. The impact of these symbols cannot be underestimated because they presented an impression of power and success for a nation that was devastated by defeat; they provided a rallying cry for a nation seeking to reestablish itself as a major power. Hitler fed the national disgrace with charges against Jews, claiming that they bore responsibility for Germany's problems. Hitler's personal hatred of Jews was consistent with the attitude of anti-Semitism that was common throughout Europe at the end of World War I.

Using this political and social climate to his advantage, Hitler, with his delusion of grandeur, plotted to seize political power. His revolution was planned for November 11, 1923, the fifth anniversary of Germany's defeat. Hitler and his mob of 3,000 failed in this attempt. He was imprisoned along with nine of his followers, but his trial created national attention, and Hitler was catapulted from being a small-time leader of a small band of rowdies and thugs to a national figure who claimed to care only for the betterment of Germany. He spent nine months in prison, but it was time well-spent for him. He polished his oratory with the captive audience of fellow prisoners and wrote a book entitled *Mein Kampf*, with the help of Rudolf Hess, who was later to become a top Nazi official. With its publication, the Nazis had another powerful symbol: the philosophical tract that articulated the anger and hatred that they would fashion into national policy.

Once he was released from prison, Hitler continued his political activities and worked to rebuild the Nazi party. The 1928 elections were a disaster for the Nazis, but Hitler persevered. As economic conditions worsened, the supporters of the Hitler fringe grew. In the 1930 elections, the Nazis received the second highest number of votes. By 1932, the Nazis received the highest count, but Hitler was defeated that year for president of the German Federal Republic by the re-election of eighty-six-year-old Paul von Hindenburg, a World War I hero and field marshal. Hindenburg had previously underestimated Hitler, but with the victory of the Nazi party in 1932, he recognized that he needed to address Hitler's growing political power. The ailing Hindenburg brought his political foe into the government and soon elevated Hitler to the position of Chancellor of Germany.

Hitler had risen to power on a platform of German superiority and racial discrimination. Hitler used the deterioration of the German economy as the fodder for his power oratory. As he extolled the superiority of the Aryan people and proposed simplistic solutions to the nation's problems, Hitler gained tremendous public support. People who simply wanted their lives to be better became believers in the promise of the Nazi party. But the promise also carried a threat: the threat to destroy anyone who did not conform to the image of Aryan superiority. Hitler's group of brown-shirted followers also gained power. It was the role of these storm troopers to harass and torment any political opposition to Hitler. They literally and figuratively beat Hitler's opponents into submission and eliminated his enemies.

In a demoralized and angry nation, a leader who extolled German superiority gained public support. The conditions were ripe for a scapegoat. Hitler's anti-Semitism provided an excellent scapegoat. Sadly, for a nation that was defeated and beleaguered, people sought someone to blame. Prior to Hitler's reign, German Jews had been active, positive contributors to German society with distinguished careers in government, education, medicine, the law, and the military. Their prominence fueled the hatred. But Jews were not the only target of this inhuman regime. Hitler's storm troopers rounded up all their foes—political opponents, Gypsies, homosexuals, Jehovah's Witnesses, trade union leaders, the handicapped, and anyone else who did not contribute to the vision of Nazi superiority.

Within three months of his appointment as chancellor, Hitler began the organized reign of terror against the German Jews which was to last until 1945. On April 1, 1933, the government-directed boycott of Jewish-owned stores and businesses began. As a result of the Civil Service Law of April 7, 1933, Jews and other non-Aryans were forced out of civil service jobs and any other positions with public visibility. This act was the first piece of legislation designed to segregate, isolate, and demoralize German Jews. Jews accounted for less than one percent of the German population, yet as the target of Hitlerian bigotry they were the victims of over 200 pieces of discriminatory legislation from the Civil Service Laws in 1933 and 1939.

Spring 1933 brought another event that marked the destruction of the free exchange of ideas in Germany. On May 10, in a frenzy, German students, teachers, and others contributed to the nazification of the culture by mounting a massive pillaging and book-burning that took place in thirty German cities. The works of authors disapproved of by the Hitler regime were ceremoniously burned. Ironically, one hundred years before this event, poet Heinrich Heine, a German Jew, had said of book-burning: "Where one burns books, one will, in the end, burn people." In 1933 these words were sadly prophetic of events to come in Germany and Eastern Europe. The burning of books was coupled with a concerted effort to shape and control public opinion through a powerful propaganda effort. Hitler recognized that he needed to eliminate those who would oppose him, to limit the citizenry's information and the right to dissent, and to provide citizens with someone or something to blame.

In 1935, German Jews were dealt another severe punishment. The Nuremberg Race Laws provided a legal justification for the Nazi persecution of the Jews. These laws stripped German Jews of their citizenship and deprived them of all of their political rights. Marriage or sexual relations between Jews and non-Jews was forbidden. A Jew was defined by ancestry regardless of religious beliefs and practices. A Jew was defined by the Nazis as anyone with three Jewish grandparents or anyone who belonged to the Jewish community after September 15, 1935 and had two Jewish grandparents. The definition was extended to anyone who married a Jew after that date and to any child either legitimate or illegitimate who was born to at least one Jewish parent. Any Jewish blood was cause for labeling people as *Mischling*, a term which meant "hybrids." A

Mischling, first degree, had two Jewish grandparents while a *Mischling*, second degree, had one Jewish grandparent (see chapter 3 on Koehn's *Mischling, Second Degree*).

The Nuremberg Laws fed public ostracism of Jews. Businesses, for example, bore signs saying Jews were not welcome and some park benches were labeled "for Jews only." The Nazis were squeezing the Jews from the social and economic mainstream of German life. The regulations continued through 1937 and 1938. All Jewish property had to be registered and 80 percent of their businesses were either seized or sold at ridiculously cheap prices. Jewish lawyers were denied the right to practice; Jewish doctors could treat only Jewish patients. As German Jews sought to escape, their passports bore the letter *J* for *Jude*.

November 9, 1938 marked a major, further deterioration of the already-difficult conditions for German Jews. In a Nazi-encouraged rampage, Germans in Austria and Sudetenland as well as in Germany used the assassination of a low-ranking official in the Paris German embassy by a seventeen-year-old Jewish man as the justification for a public assault on Jews and their synagogues. This pogrom, called *Kristallnacht* ("crystal night," or "night of broken glass") saw the murder of ninety-six Jews, the destruction of over 1,000 synagogues, and the looting of over 7,000 businesses. Thirty thousand Jews, mostly men, were arrested, while numerous Jewish cemeteries, hospitals, and homes were destroyed. The concentration camps at Dachau and Buchenwald were expanded to accommodate the newly incarcerated as the first wave of systematic arrests of Austrian and German Jews began.

From the earliest days of Hitler's empire, called the Third Reich, the Nazis began to construct camps where they would imprison their enemies. Dachau was established in 1933; Sachsenhausen in 1936; Buchenwald in 1938; Mauthausen and Flossenburg in 1938; and Ravensbruck women's prison in 1939. By the beginning of World War II when Germany invaded Poland and set up new camps, the network of camps was established. They would play a vital part in Germany's war efforts, either as work camps where slave labor fueled the Nazi war machine or as death camps where the Nazis destroyed their enemies.

In September 1941, another action was taken against all Jews in Germany and its occupied territories. Jews over the age of six years were required to wear a yellow Star of David badge in public. This act symbolically completed the identification and isolation of European Jews. While the murder of those perceived by Hitler and his inner circle to be enemies had been an ongoing act since 1933, there is no indication that they planned to try to kill all European Jews until 1941 and the invasion of Russia. In January 1942 the Nazi hierarchy met in Berlin for the now infamous Wannsee Conference, where the "Final Solution" was planned and discussed. This was the plan to kill all Jews living in Europe. While the Nazis abused and murdered members of a number of religious, social, and political groups whom they considered enemies, the "Final Solution" focused on Jews. From 1941 to 1945, as Germany tried to capture the free world, the assault against European Jews was stepped up.

In 1945 the defeat of the Third Reich ended the Second World War and the camps were liberated, but European Jews continued to struggle. For the survivors, few had homes or jobs or family to return to; their pre-Nazi lives were shattered and few of the fragments even remained. True survival for them was to create new lives and to establish a home where they could be safe and free. While the physical horrors these people suffered can be recounted, the mental anguish and the psychological torture of their persecution created scars that time can diminish, but cannot totally heal. The fate of the Jewish population and the stories of the Holocaust—the ghettos, the hiding, the camps, the escape, the survival, and the triumph of the human spirit—are revealed in the literature of their experiences.

Lessons from the Holocaust provide us with a framework to view ongoing atrocities. Current world conditions reaffirm the need to be vigilant. Events in places such as China, Iraq, Cambodia, Haiti, and Iran remind us that the fragility of human life may be exceeded only by the inhumanity of despots. In recent history, we have witnessed atrocities around the world in places like Cambodia, Rwanda, and Bosnia, among others. The slaughter in these countries is more than political differences or tribal wars; it is genocide. These events and the talk of "ethnic cleansing" remind us of the words of philosopher George Santayana: "Those who cannot remember the past are condemned to repeat it." The magnitude of atrocities, whether in Hitler's Third Reich or current trouble spots in the world, challenges the imagination and conscience of rational people everywhere because we find these actions both unbelievable and unspeakable. Yet the evidence is as irrefutable as it is unforgettable.

It is easy to look at these locales and assume that these affronts to humanity don't happen here; however, the American press regularly reports the actions of hate groups, such as the Ku Klux Klan. We also have witnessed the escalation of hate crimes, such as the desecration of synagogues, vandalism of Jewish cemeteries, and discrimination against Jews in our society. It *does* happen here and we must be ever vigilant against hate mongers. We must be concerned about the rise in neo-Nazi groups here and in Europe, because while they are individuals festering with hate, they are also followers of Adolf Hitler and his doctrine of murder and destruction.

Teachers, parents, youth leaders, and others in positions of influence have a special responsibility to see that subsequent generations never forget what happened in Europe between 1933 and 1945. To that end, this book is designed to provide them with resources to help young people come to an awareness of the magnitude of the Holocaust and to put a human face on the atrocities.

A number of events, including the opening of the United States Holocaust Memorial Museum in Washington, D.C., the release of Steven Spielberg's film, *Schlinder's List*, and the 50th anniversary of the end of World War II and the liberation of the camps, have revitalized the concern of thoughtful adults that today's young people must learn about this terrible time. Reading and experiencing literature of the Holocaust, especially those books either by or about young people, will provide them with powerful insights about the realities of the period. An inherent value of literature is its ability to transport readers to different times and different circumstances than those that they have experienced. Through literature, readers can make personal connections with those characters, real and fictional, who lived or died during the period of the Holocaust.

The experience of reading heightens awareness by evoking both empathetic or sympathetic responses from readers. This need for a heightened awareness was addressed by the National Council of Teachers of English (NCTE) at the fall 1993 conference in Pittsburgh where it adopted the following resolution, *On Teaching About Intolerance and Genocide:*

> BACKGROUND: The teachers who proposed this resolution cited a 1993 Roper survey which showed that 22 percent of students and 20 percent of adults responding to the survey believed there was a possibility that the European Holocaust of the 1930s and 1940s did not happen. The teachers said the survey underscored the need for vigilance against bigotry and genocide, and attempts to "revise" historical fact.
>
> Proponents said acts of racial, ethnic, class, and religious hostility are increasing in numbers around the world, and that the destructive forces of intolerance must be countered in every setting. Education, they said, is the most powerful tool to help students perceive others' victimization and to prepare them to fight intolerance. The resolution's proponents believe students should study the wealth of primary source material by, as well as literature about, the victims of intolerance.
>
> RESOLVED, that the National Council of Teachers of English affirm that students should read and discuss literature on genocide and intolerance within an historically accurate framework with special emphasis on primary source material; and that NCTE create a task force to submit for publication a compilation of resources including visual media, literature, and agencies that can assist teachers in planning and producing instructional materials on the rhetoric and literature of genocide and intolerance.

We live in violent and unsettled times. Children and young people are constantly reminded by the media of the tenuous nature of life on the streets. Critics say that our youth are deadened to the pain that violence breeds. We, as responsible adults, need to awaken a sense of revulsion and horror for all acts of violence and destruction. The Nazis' systematic, maniacal attempt to destroy European Jews and others provides today's young people with a graphic and frightening awareness of the power of violence. While events that occurred over fifty years ago in Europe may seem to be distant and unbelievable history for today's young people, the horror of these events cannot be ignored or forgotten if civilization is to endure. Each succeeding generation must know the horror and say "Not again; not in our time." Only then will we be assured that the darkness that Elie Wiesel describes will not fall over our civilization again. Wiesel wrote of the Holocaust: "In those times there was darkness everywhere. In heaven and on earth, all the gates of compassion seemed to have been closed. The killer killed and the Jews died and the outside world adopted an attitude either of complicity or of indifference. Only a few had the courage to care." (Meltzer, *Rescue*, p.12). As the magnitude and truth of the Holocaust became part of the world's consciousness, a horrified world said "Never Again," words that need to be echoed by every generation.

References

Adler, David A. *We Remember the Holocaust*. Henry Holt, 1989.

Bachrach, Susan D. *Tell Them We Remember: The Story of the Holocaust*. Little, Brown, 1994.

Berenbaum, Michael. Arnold Kramer, photography editor. *The World Must Know: The History of the Holocaust as Told in the United States Holocaust Memorial Museum*. Little, Brown, 1993.

Chaikin, Miriam. *A Nightmare in History: The Holocaust 1933-1945*. Clarion Books, 1987.

Lawless, Charles. *. . . and God Cried: The Holocaust Remembered*. Wieser & Wieser, 1994.

Meltzer, Milton. *Never to Forget: The Jews of the Holocaust*. Harper & Row, 1976.

Meltzer, Milton. *Rescue: The Story of How Gentiles Saved Jews in the Holocaust*. HarperCollins, 1988.

"The Holocaust FAQ, 1933–435," prepared by Simon Wiesenthal Center Library and Archives, 1994.

"The Holocaust: An Historical Summary." United States Holocaust Memorial Museum (no date).

2

It Really Happened

Informational Books, Photo Essays, Maps

> It is far more important that these incredible events be
> established by clear and public proof, so that no one can
> ever doubt that they were fact and not fable.
>
> Brig. Gen. Telford Taylor, U.S. Army, from
> *We Remember the Holocaust*

This chapter presents informational books and photographic essays that provide youthful readers with factual accounts of the Holocaust. From 1933 to 1945 six million Jews died as a part of Adolf Hitler's "Final Solution," while five million other people deemed "undesirables" were also killed. The numerical facts and events of the times are shocking and frightening. Informational books provide youthful readers with the factual background and a context in which to examine what occurred. It helps them to gain a perspective on the times in which these events took place. Reasonable people can never look to that period without asking "Why did these atrocities happen?" and "How could they have happened?" While there may never be fully satisfactory explanations for the actions of Hitler and his followers, informational books help readers to begin to understand the times. Such books also answer revisionists who seek to minimize both the events of the Holocaust and their impact.

The stark reality of the facts, supported by photographs, provides readers with a context to comprehend the magnitude of the horrors. Included in this chapter are books that provide brief histories of anti-Semitism, descriptions of the events from 1933 to 1945, real experiences of those who witnessed and survived the Holocaust, and collections of archival photographs of the times. Suggestions for using these books are also included.

Prior to Reading: Think About . . .

Young people need to do some preliminary thinking and talking to prepare them to understand what they read or what is read to them about the Holocaust. They need opportunities to ask questions and to raise issues and concerns. The following questions can be used to prompt this discussion:

- What do you already know about the Holocaust? Hitler? Nazism? Where did you get this information?

- What things are you interested in learning about the Holocaust? What questions do you have about it?

- The Holocaust happened before you were born. Why do you think you need to learn about it now?

- Describe an experience you have had with prejudice, either when you were biased against someone else or when someone discriminated against you. Role play these experiences with classmates. What did you learn from these experiences?

- Read the quotations listed from the book you have chosen to read (or the book that will be read to you.) What do you think they mean? What do you think they reveal about the contents of the book?

Focus: It Really Happened

An Album of Nazism by William Loren Katz. (JM, S)

The Artists of Terezin by Gerald Green, with illustrations by the inmates of Terezin. (S, JM)

The Children We Remember by Chana Byers Abells. (AL)

The Holocaust: The Fire That Raged by Seymour Rossel. (E, JM)

Never to Forget: The Jews of the Holocaust by Milton Meltzer. (S, JM)

A Nightmare in History: The Holocaust 1933–1945 by Miriam Chaikin. (JM, S)

The Number on My Grandfather's Arm by David A. Adler. (P, E)

Remember Not to Forget: A Memory of the Holocaust by Norman H. Finkelstein. (E, P)

Smoke and Ashes: The Story of the Holocaust by Barbara Rogasky. (JM, S)

Tell Them We Remember: The Story of the Holocaust by Susan D. Bachrach. (JM, E, S)

The Warsaw Ghetto Uprising by Karen Zeinert. (E, JM)

We Remember the Holocaust by David A. Adler. (JM, S)

The World Must Know. The History of the Holocaust as Told in the United States Holocaust Memorial Museum by Michael Berenbaum. Arnold Kramer, photography editor. (S, JM)

All School Levels

Abells, Chana Byers. *The Children We Remember.* Greenwillow Books, 1983, 1986. 45 pages.

The Nazis hated the children because they were Jews. (unnumbered)

At a Glance ▪ Deceptively simple, this photo essay is appropriate for all ages. Photographs from the Yad Vashem Archives in Jerusalem accompanied by a brief text depict Jewish children who lived and died during the Holocaust.

Summary ▪ Chana Byers Abells creates a poignant, yet unsensationalized photographic perspective. Through moving photographs and sparse text, Abells, director of the photo and film division of the Yad Vashem Archives, recreates what daily life was like for Jewish children and their families. In fewer than fifty pages, the reader is able to identify with the children in the photographs, first prior to the rise of Nazism and then during the Nazi reign of terror. This is a powerful book that evokes a wide range of emotions.

But some children survived. (unnumbered)

Teaching Considerations ▪ Allow students ample time to examine and discuss the photographs. Have students describe what they think may have happened before a photograph was taken and what might happen after it was taken. Often these photographs give rise to many questions and concerns. Give younger students opportunities to draw what they are feeling. Older students can use writing to describe what they see and what they feel. This book can be used effectively as a springboard to the other informational books described in this chapter. Seymour Rossel's instructional text, *The Holocaust: The World and the Jews, 1933–1946* (see chapter 7), provides students with information on how to examine photographs to learn about the Holocaust.

Primary School Level

Adler, David A. *The Number on My Grandfather's Arm.* UAHC Press, 1987. 28 pages.

I followed Grandpa and sat next to him on the couch. "I'll tell you about the number," Grandpa said. (p. 10)

At a Glance ▪ A Jewish grandfather tells his young granddaughter about life under Hitler. This book could be read to primary age children. It is also appropriate for elementary school children.

Summary ▪ David Adler tells of this frightening period in history in language that young children can understand. Without being exploited or minimized, the terrifying nature of the Holocaust is told through the vehicle of a loving relationship between a girl and her grandfather. In the story, a seven-year-old girl learns of her grandfather's experiences as a survivor of the Holocaust. He explains to her what happened to the Jewish people in Europe while Hitler was in power. He shows her the number tattooed on his arm and describes the concentration camps. The simple text is enhanced by contemporary photographs of the girl and her grandfather talking to each other interspersed with archival photographs.

> There were tears in Grandpa's eyes and in my eyes, too. "I was one of the lucky ones," Grandpa said. "I survived." (p. 21)

Teaching Considerations ▪ Introduce this book by giving children an opportunity to talk about their own grandparents. Have them remember a family story that they heard from a grandparent or other older family member. Invite Holocaust survivors from your community to visit the classroom. Ask them to talk informally about their families with the students. Have a map and timeline available for them to use as they tell of their experiences. These can also then be related to the book to help place it within an historical context. David Adler's book, *A Picture Book of Anne Frank* (see chapter 3), and Levey Oppenheim's book, *The Lily Cupboard,* are appropriate follow-up books.

Additional Titles: Primary School Level

The Children We Remember by Chana Byers Abells. (AL)

Remember Not to Forget: A Memory of the Holocaust by Norman H. Finkelstein. (E)

Elementary School Level

Finkelstein, Norman H. Illustrated by Lois and Lars Hokanson. *Remember Not to Forget, A Memory of the Holocaust.* Franklin Watts, 1985. 31 pages.

> Between 1933 and 1945 six million Jewish men, women and children were murdered in Germany and other European countries. . . . They died for only one reason: they were Jewish.
>
> How could such a thing have happened? To answer this question, we must look far back in history. (p. 7)

At a Glance ▪ This book presents a brief overview of the Holocaust, the conditions preceding it, and events since that time. Less than thirty pages in length, it is appropriate for elementary school children. It could also be read to primary school-age children.

Summary ▪ Accompanied by woodcut illustrations, Norman Finkelstein presents a brief history of anti-Semitism in an attempt to explain the conditions that allowed the Holocaust to happen. Life for Jewish people under Nazism resulting in the deaths of over two-thirds of Europe's Jews is described. The birth of Israel after World War II; the subsequent establishment of Yad Vashem, the national institution to study and research the Holocaust; and Holocaust Remembrance Day are also explained.

> People saw the need to keep the memory of the Holo-caust alive in order to prevent such a catastrophe from happening again. (p. 25)

Teaching Considerations ▪ While this book is short, it is replete with facts that students will need to internalize and to reflect upon. Help students to read the book in segments and discuss the information with them. Students can then develop a fact chart or matrix listing the basic information they learned from this book. This book can be used effectively in conjunction with *The Children We Remember* by Chana Byers Abells (see entry in this chapter) and *The Big Lie, A True Story* by Isabella Leitner (see chapter 3). It also can be used as an introduction to the more extensive coverage of the Holocaust in Rossel's book, *The Holocaust: The Fire That Raged* (see following).

Rossel, Seymour. *The Holocaust: The Fire That Raged.* Franklin Watts, 1989. 124 pages.

> Using the Jews as a scapegoat—a group that could be blamed for any problem—is called *anti-Semitism.* Adolf Hitler believed that he could use anti-Semitism as a tool to help him become more popular. (p. 17)

At a Glance ▪ Seymour Rossel's book presents an overview of the Holocaust from the conditions after World War I that led to the rise of Hitler to the trials after World War II. Accompanied by photographs and written in a clear, easy-to-understand style, this book is appropriate for elementary and junior high/middle school students.

Summary ▪ This book is designed to answer the three questions most frequently asked about the Holocaust: What happened? How did we let it happen? Could it happen again? Divided into eleven chapters, it begins with information about the Treaty of Versailles and social and economic conditions in Germany following World War I. The rise of Hitler and the Nazi party and the manipulation of the population against the Jews are described as well as the Nuremberg Laws and *Kristallnacht*. The conquest of Europe and the establishment of the ghettos and camps leading to the efforts to implement the "Final Solution" are also described. Attempts by Jews to escape and revolt are discussed as well as why these attempts were not more widespread or successful. Attempts to rescue Jews as well as the inaction of many governments are also discussed. The book concludes with the defeat of Germany and the subsequent trials of major Nazi figures. The last chapter defines genocide and explores what we must do to ensure that there is never again another Holocaust. A chronology of the Holocaust and recommended sources for further reading are also included.

> We must all look into our hearts. Would we let our neighbors be taken without speaking out? Would we let them be put to death without trying to rescue them? Would we let another Holocaust happen? (p. 106)

Teaching Considerations ▪ This book lends itself well to reading aloud to students and stimulating discussion and to simple notetaking. Students can develop timelines showing the major events of the Holocaust, and they can design ways to answer the three questions posed by the book. To help them understand the human dimensions of the Holocaust, provide them with biographies and personal narratives from chapter 3. Eve Bunting's powerful picture book, *Terrible Things,* can be used to explore the implications of scapegoating and personal responsibility. Rossel's text, *The Holocaust: The World and the Jews, 1933–45,* serves as an excellent companion to this book (see chapter 7).

Zeinert, Karen. *The Warsaw Ghetto Uprising.* Millbrook Press, 1993. 112 pages.

> The uprising in Warsaw was the first in any city under Nazi control, and it had great impact. (p. 89)

For Jews in death camps and other ghettos, the news of the Warsaw uprising was inspiring. If the Jews in Warsaw could fight, they said, they could do the same. Revolts broke out in other ghettos and even in death camps, including Treblinka. (p. 90)

At a Glance ▪ Zeinert's book presents an overview of the uprising of Poland's Warsaw Ghetto, from the conditions leading up to it to the aftermath. The text is written in a clear, easy to understand style, and is enhanced by photos. It is appropriate for elementary school level students and junior high/middle school students.

Summary ▪ When the Germans invaded Poland in 1939, more than three million Jews lived in that country. When the war was over, 90 percent of them were dead. Jewish people lived throughout Poland, and 300,000 of them lived in Warsaw, a city with a population of one million. With the German invasion, many more Jews fled to Warsaw, where they thought they would be safe. A few months after Warsaw was captured, the Jews were ordered to wear identifying armbands. A little more than a year after the invasion, they were forced to move into the ghetto where conditions steadily deteriorated. Various factions within the ghetto urged the people to revolt, but others thought survival was ensured as long as they provided labor for the Germans. In the summer of 1942, the Germans began deporting Jews from the ghetto to what were called work camps. Planning for armed resistance increased, and when confirmation reached the ghetto in 1943 that the deportations were to death camps, the uprising began. With limited weapons, the Jews battled heroically. Although they were ultimately defeated and the Warsaw Ghetto reduced to a pile of rubble, their rebellion inspired defiance in and resistance by others under Nazi control.

"Whether we could obtain weapons or not, we owed it to ourselves to resist, with bare hands if necessary. We could do at least some damage to the Germans by setting fire to the factories . . . inside the ghetto." (Milton Meltzer, p. 58.)

Teaching Considerations ▪ At a time in our society when young people look to Hollywood or professional sports figures for their heroes, this book provides teachers with an opportunity to examine the concept of true heroism with their students. The events in the

Warsaw Ghetto surpass any action movie of today as real examples of sheer guts and determination. This book lends itself well to being read aloud to students. Elementary school students will benefit from additional historical context and explanation by the teacher as well as discussion to clarify what they are learning. It is more important for them to develop an overall sense of what occurred and its implications than to master the various names and details. Junior high/middle school students can use this book as a springboard to learning more about specific aspects of the uprising or the individuals involved. The events of the uprising could be used for dramatization with older students. The documentary video, *The Warsaw Ghetto*, can be used with junior high/middle school students (see chapter 7). Uri Orlev's novel, *The Man from the Other Side*, based on the true experiences of a Polish journalist, is appropriate for junior high/middle school students (see chapter 4). Elementary school children can learn more from *Jacob's Rescue* by Malka Drucker and Michael Halperin (see chapter 3).

Additional Titles: Elementary School Level

The Children We Remember by Chana Byers Abells. (AL)

The Number on My Grandfather's Arm by David A. Adler. (P)

Tell Them We Remember: The Story of the Holocaust by Susan D. Bachrach. (JM)

Junior High/Middle School Level

Adler, David A. *We Remember the Holocaust.* Henry Holt, 1989. 148 pages.

This book began as a history, but I wanted my son to know more than names, dates, places, a tally of the people killed. I wanted him to learn about the Holocaust not only within its historical context, but also as the Jews of Europe knew it, as one personal tragedy on top of another. (p. viii)

At a Glance ▪ This book is a powerful introduction to the Holocaust with historical events personalized by photographs and the memories of young people who witnessed and survived its horrors. It provides an excellent introduction to the Holocaust for junior high/middle school students and would also be appropriate for some secondary school students.

Summary ▪ David Adler, author of many books for young people, makes history come alive by telling the events from 1933 to 1945 through the voices of the children and young people who lived them. These young people describe life after World War I during the rise of Hitler and Nazism. Their personal remembrances and photographs chronicle daily events as one freedom after another is taken away from the Jewish people. Life and death in the ghettos and prison camps are painfully described by those who witnessed terrible events and survived them. Yet Adler ends the book on a hopeful note: that by remembering the past, we will not be condemned to live it again. A chronology of important dates from 1933 to 1945 and a glossary add to the usefulness of this book. It is a 1989 Notable Children's Trade Book in Social Studies.

> People today must learn not to hate, to teach their children not to hate. They must understand that hatred can lead to discrimination and violence. What happened once must not happen again. (p. 103)

Teaching Considerations ▪ This book lends itself well to being read aloud to a class. It is a valuable one to keep in the classroom as students like to turn to it frequently to look at the photographs, reread sections, and check out dates and facts. It can also serve as a springboard for researching topics suggested in the book. This book generally prompts student interest in learning more about specific people who lived during the time of the Holocaust. Provide them with biographies and personal narratives from chapter 3. Have students interview someone who was growing up during the period from 1933 to 1945. Ask them to describe their lives at that time. Compare these stories with those in the book.

Bachrach, Susan D. *Tell Them We Remember: The Story of the Holocaust.* Little, Brown, 1994. 112 pages.

Schools also played an important role in spreading Nazi ideas. While some books were removed from classrooms by censors, other textbooks, newly written, were brought in to teach students a blind obedience to the party, love for Hitler, and antisemitism. (p. 16)

At a Glance ▪ Published in conjunction with the United States Holocaust Memorial Museum, this book, through text and photographs, helps the reader to understand how the lives of children and young people were affected by the Holocaust. It is appropriate for junior high/middle school students and for some secondary school students. It also could be read to elementary school-age children.

Summary ▪ Accompanying a description of the major historical events of the Holocaust are glimpses of the individual experiences of twenty children and young people during this time. While most of them are Jews, some are representative of other groups persecuted by the Nazis. This format successfully personalizes this terrible time and its impact on innocent people. The text consists of three parts: Nazi Germany; the "Final Solution"; and Rescue, Resistance, and Liberation. It also has a chronology of major events, a glossary of important terms, suggestions for further reading, and numerous compelling photographs.

> Anyone who had three or four Jewish grandparents was defined as a Jew, regardless of whether that individual identified himself or herself as a Jew or belonged to the Jewish religious community. Many Germans who had not practiced Judaism for years found themselves caught in the grip of Nazi terror. Even people with Jewish grandparents who had converted to Christianity were defined as Jews. (p. 18)

Teaching Considerations ▪ This book provides teachers with an excellent resource for introducing students to the Holocaust and its impact on children and young adults. It would make a valuable addition to a classroom library so that students could refer to it frequently. The vignettes could be used as a springboard to reading memoirs and biographies of other young people (see entries in chapter 3). Information on films/videos and audio recordings is given in chapter 7. Have students select a particular event of the Holocaust and do a study of it by reading at least three other accounts and then sharing their findings with the class.

Chaikin, Miriam. *A Nightmare in History: The Holocaust 1933–1945.* Clarion Books, 1987. 150 pages.

The twelve years in which Hitler was in power were a nightmare in history. (p. 3)

At a Glance ▪ This book describes the history of anti-Semitism and how the Nazis sought to make all of Europe *Judenrein*—a place without Jews. It provides a combination of historical data and personal experiences. It is appropriate for junior high/middle school students and some secondary school students.

Summary ▪ In her introduction, Miriam Chaikin states that she wrote her book to keep alive for memory's sake how the Nazi machinery annihilated six million Jews. She offers a brief history of the Jewish people, their relationship to Christianity, and the growth of prejudice against Jewish people throughout the years. Accounts of individual experiences and excerpts from diaries help to personalize the historical events. The roles that specific individuals as well as the various nations of the world played in helping or refusing to help the Jews during the Holocaust is also described.

Six million. Behind each digit, starting with the number one, was a pair of eyes, a face, a living, vital human being. (p. 137)

Teaching Considerations ▪ Students can develop a fact chart or matrix listing the basic information they learned from this book. Also, they can be helped to discuss the factors that created anti-Semitism. Have them compare these with factors that cause people to be prejudiced against other groups in our society today. This book can be used effectively in conjunction with Adler's *We Remember the Holocaust* and Bachrach's *Tell Them We Remember: The Story of the Holocaust*. The film, *About the Holocaust*, could be shown as a follow-up to this book (see chapter 7).

Katz, William Loren. *An Album of Nazism.* Franklin Watts, 1979. 90 pages.

Hitler said people "more readily fall victim to the big lie than the small lie." (p. 23)

At a Glance ▪ This pictorial history depicts in words and images the vicious regime of Adolf Hitler. While it is appropriate for junior high/middle school students, it could also be used with some secondary students.

Summary ▪ This account of Hitler's regime is replete with authentic photographs from the period. It traces Hitler's rise and concludes with the admonishment that we must never let Nazism surface again. Katz presents one- to two-page accounts of events, people, or ideas from the period and then juxtaposes photographs to the text. One of the most effective sections of the book, on the Wallacchs of Munich, Germany, puts a human face on the Holocaust.

> In 1945 the U.S. prosecutor at the Nuremberg war trials was Supreme Court Justice Robert Jackson. He told the court: "The wrongs we seek to condemn and punish have been so calculated, so malignant and so devastating, that civilization cannot tolerate their being ignored because it cannot survive their being repeated." (p. 84)

Teaching Considerations ▪ Ask students to select a photograph and create a framework for it by imagining that they have taken it. What was happening beyond the lens? How did they feel at the time? What were the conditions? This book can be used effectively in conjunction with *The Children We Remember* by Chana Byers Abells and David A. Adler's *We Remember the Holocaust*. It can also be used as a springboard for researching topics and issues raised in the book. The film, *The Life of Adolf Hitler*, may be shown in conjunction with this book (see chapter 7). Additionally, Seymour Rossel's text, *The Holocaust: The World and the Jews, 1933–1946*, provides students with information on how to examine photographs and to read offical documents and eyewitness accounts to learn about the Holocaust (see chapter 7).

Rogasky, Barbara. *Smoke and Ashes: The Story of the Holocaust.* Holiday House, 1988. 187 pages.

> The seeds of misunderstanding, ignorance and hate were sown long before Hitler. The Nazis would not have been able to succeed in their work of destruction if the foundation had not been formed centuries earlier. (p. 10)

At a Glance ▪ This well-illustrated account captures the experience of the Holocaust years. It is an appropriate introduction for junior high/middle school students and for some secondary school students.

Summary ▪ Rogasky provides an excellent primer for students seeking initial information about the Holocaust and its causes. She also traces the conditions in the ghettos and in the camps and the efforts to combat the Nazis by individual acts or by organized acts of the Resistance. She concludes the book with present-day examples of racist hate crimes. The photographs are powerful depictions of the times.

> To remember the Holocaust, to remember the step-by-step growth of that monstrous machinery of destruction, is to help prevent the flowering of some new and possibly even greater evil. (p. 180)

Teaching Considerations ▪ This book provides basic information that students can compile in the form of graphic organizers such as fact charts, matrices, or cognitive maps. It can also be used as a starting point for further research on efforts to save Jews. Meltzer's *Rescue: The Story of How Gentiles Saved Jews in the Holocaust* and Rosenberg's *Hiding to Survive: Stories of Jewish Children Rescued from the Holocaust* can be used in conjunction with this book (see chapter 3). The film, *Triumph of Memory,* could be shown to both junior high/middle school and secondary students; *Flames in the Ashes* is more appropriate for secondary students (see chapter 7). Have students develop, individually or in small groups, presentations that focus on why it is important to remember this historical period and what humankind must learn from the Holocaust.

Additional Titles: Junior High/ Middle School Level

The Artists of Terezin by Gerald Green, with illustrations by the inmates of Terezin. (S)

The Children We Remember by Chana Byers Abells. (AL)

The Holocaust: The Fire That Raged by Seymour Rossel. (E)

Never to Forget: The Jews of the Holocaust by Milton Meltzer. (S)

The Warsaw Ghetto Uprising by Karen Zeinert. (E)

The World Must Know: The History of the Holocaust as Told in the United States Holocaust Memorial Museum by Michael Berenbaum. Arnold Kramer, photography editor. (S)

Secondary School Level

Berenbaum, Michael. Arnold Kramer, photography editor. *The World Must Know: The History of the Holocaust as Told in the United States Holocaust Memorial Museum.* Little, Brown, 1993. 240 pages.

> Unquestionably, there is a great measure of truth in the caveat that only a survivor of the Holocaust can fully know and understand what happened in those terrible years, but the world has to know the story of the Holocaust, the story has to be remembered, and in order to be remembered it has to be seen—and told. (p. xv)

At a Glance ▪ Published in conjunction with the opening of the United States Holocaust Memorial Museum, this book, through words and photographs, provides the reader with a comprehensive survey of the Holocaust. It is appropriate for secondary students, some junior high/middle school students, and teachers of all levels.

Summary ▪ Written by the project director of the U.S. Holocaust Memorial Museum, this book draws upon its extensive resources, including eyewitness accounts, photographs, and artifacts. It provides a comprehensive historical overview of this era and tells the human stories from pre-Holocaust days through its aftermath as well. These are the stories of those who perpetrated the Holocaust, those who passively let it happen, those who were its intended victims, and those who attempted to help others survive the horrors of the times.

> I have told you this story not to weaken you
> But to strengthen you.
> Now it is up to you. Camp prisoner (pp. 3, 223)

Teaching Considerations ▪ This book is compelling reading and is a valuable addition to a classroom library. While it can be used in conjunction with a visit to the U.S. Holocaust Memorial Museum, it also stands alone on its own merits. It can provide an information base for students and a springboard for further individual research. Additional information can be obtained from reading . . . *and God Cried: The Holocaust Remembered* by Charles Lawless in this chapter. Students can read about non-Jews who were systematically persecuted by the Nazis in Friedman's *The Other Victims, First-Person Stories of Non-Jews Persecuted by the Nazis* and Ramati's *And the Violins Stopped Playing: A Story of the Gypsy Holocaust* (see chapter 3). Students might also locate other Holocaust museums or educational centers near where they live and arrange a visitation (see chapter 7 for more information). Class discussion could focus on why there is a need for these facilities and their mission.

Green, Gerald, with illustrations by the inmates of Terezin. *The Artists of Terezin.* Hawthorn Books, 1969. 187 pages.

> I'm impelled to speculate that the Terezin fraud, this model ghetto, this old folks' home with its phony stores and fake coffee shop, its concerts and theater, was in part a product of this imperfectly understood suspicion on the part of some Nazis that they were nothing more than a gang of wicked bastards, for whom punishment was inevitable. The truly outrageous thing is that Terezin worked marvelously for them. It deceived its inmates. It prolonged the deception of many neutrals and many in the West. And although in this last function it may be said ultimately to have failed, it was utilized as an earnest model of humanitarianism by the Nazi leaders to the very end. (pp. 26–27)

At a Glance ▪ Over 100 paintings and drawings done by inmates of the Terezin "model" concentration camp are included in this account of the experiences of this camp. This book is appropriate for secondary students and some junior high/middle school students as well.

Summary ▪ The Nazis used the camp at Terezin as a model camp and as a front to hide the true atrocities that were taking place in other camps. The Nazis allowed inspections of Terezin. The inmates were able to bring forty pounds of personal belongings with them into the camp and to stay with their families. For many of the Jews, the relatively relaxed regulations at this camp allowed them to bring paints, books, and writing materials with them. While Terezin masqueraded as a model camp, it was really a collection spot for Jews to be sent "East," meaning to death camps. While the inmates were there, the Nazis did allow them to practice their art, but only as long as it did not reveal the reality of their lives at Terezin. When the artists and writers were too honest, they were silenced and often beaten to death. While Terezin was not a death camp—that is, there was not a systematic plan to kill the inmates—nearly one-fourth of all the inmates died there of starvation, ill-treatment and beatings, or other causes. But some of the art endured, and it speaks to the perseverance of the human spirit as it rejects the basest kinds of inhumanity.

> When [Joseph] Conrad wrote that the artist "speaks to our capacity for delight and wonder, to the sense of mystery surrounding our lives; to our sense of pity, and beauty and pain," he might have been writing about the artists of Terezin. Pity, beauty, and pain. (p. 159)

Teaching Considerations ▪ Artists responded to the horrors of the Holocaust through drawings and paintings. Have students examine paintings from the times and discuss their impact. Have them respond in writing to the saying: "A picture is worth a thousand words." Ask students: Beyond providing a human record of the treatment of the Jews, what role did the drawings, paintings, literature, and musical performances that Green describes in *The Artists of Terezin* play in the lives of the inmates? Bernbaum's *My Brother's Keeper: The Holocaust Through the Eyes of an Artist*; Fluek's *Memories of My Life in a Polish Village, 1930–1949*; and Toll's *Behind the Secret Window, A Memoir of a Hidden Childhood During World War Two* can be used as follow-up books (see chapter 3).

Meltzer, Milton. *Never to Forget: The Jews of the Holocaust.* Harper & Row, 1976. 217 pages.

> I do not believe that the world of Hitler was totally alien to the world we know. Still, before we can compare Hitler's Germany to anything else, we need to find out what it was like and how it came to be. (p. xvi)

At a Glance ▪ A National Jewish Book Award winner, this book presents an historical examination of the roots of anti-Semitism, the rise of Hitler, and the attempted total annihilation of the European Jews. It is appropriate for secondary students and some junior high/middle school students too.

Summary ▪ Milton Meltzer's highly readable historical account of the Holocaust is divided into three parts. Each part is enriched by the personal experiences of individual Jews through their diaries, journals, letters, poems, and songs. Book One, "History of Hatred," explains the conditions that led to the rise of Hitler and Nazism and the roots of the official policy of anti-Semitism in Germany. Book Two, "Destruction of the Jews," describes such infamous events as *Kristallnacht*, the massacres by mobile killing squads, the sealings of the ghettos, and the "Final Solution to the Jewish Problem"—the death camps. The final part, Book Three, "Spirit of Resistance," depicts the various forms that resistance to Nazism took among the Jewish people.

> Indifference is the greatest sin. It can become as powerful as an action. Not to do something against evil is to participate in the evil. (p. 192)

Teaching Considerations ▪ Meltzer's book is rich with information and is a valuable addition to a classroom library. It can be used to provide an information base for students and as a springboard for further individual research. The film *Shoah* can be shown along with this book (see chapter 7). Berenbaum and Kramer's *The World Must Know: The History of the Holocaust as Told in the United States Holocaust Memorial Museum* is an effective companion to this book. As a follow-up, some students may want to read Meltzer's book, *Rescue: The Story of How Gentiles Saved Jews in the Holocaust*, discussed in chapter 3. Using the quote cited above from p. 192, have students explain it by providing examples from both the 1933–45 period and some other specific historical period.

Additional Titles: Secondary School Level

An Album of Nazism by William Loren Katz. (JM)

The Children We Remember by Chana Byers Abells. (AL)

A Nightmare in History: The Holocaust 1933–1945 by Miriam Chaikin. (JM)

Smoke and Ashes: The Story of the Holocaust by Barbara Rogasky. (JM)

Tell Them We Remember: The Story of the Holocaust by Susan D. Bachrach. (JM)

We Remember the Holocaust by David A. Adler. (JM)

Further Reading for All Levels

Dwork, Deborah. *Children with a Star: Jewish Youth in Nazi Europe.* Yale University Press, 1991. 354 pages. (S)

Only 11 percent of European Jewish children alive in 1939 survived the war. Carefully researched and based on hundreds of survivor accounts and primary documents, this book describes the life experiences of Jewish children during the Holocaust. It is divided into four parts: life at home and in hiding; transit camps and ghettos; death and slave labor camps; and the aftermath of the war.

Friedrich, Otto. *The Kingdom of Auschwitz.* HarperCollins, 1982, 1994. 112 pages. (S)

For many people the word *Auschwitz* is synonymous with the Holocaust, for they believe that it was the only site of Nazi murders. While that is a painfully naive and narrow perspective, Auschwitz was the setting of unspeakable carnage. This book, which has a strong factual basis, presents an account of the camp and the horrors that occurred there. It is probably most appropriate for students in secondary schools.

Gilbert, Martin. *The Holocaust: Maps and Photographs.* Farrar, Straus, & Giroux, 1978. 59 pages. (S, JM)

This brief but powerful atlas, consisting of black-and-white archival photographs and maps, documents Jewish life in Europe prior to the Holocaust and the Nazi attempts to destroy it. Documentation is provided on the fate of non-Jewish victims, also. This reference is an excellent accompaniment to more detailed informational books for secondary students and mature junior high/middle school students. Some of the photographs are graphic in the horrors they portray.

Grossman, Mendel. *With a Camera in the Ghetto*. Ghetto Fighters' House and Hakibbutz Hameuchad Publishing House, 1970, 1972; Schocken Books, 1977. 107 pages. (S, JM)

Mendel Grossman, a gifted artist and photographer, chronicled the horrors of life in the Lodz Ghetto from 1941–1944 with his photography. His primary purpose was to leave to the world a tangible testimony of the suffering inflicted on the people. Grossman perished in 1944 at 32 years of age, but he had hidden his negatives in tin cans which his sister retrieved when the war ended. The photographs in this book are accompanied by brief explanations from his notes.

Gutman, Israel. *Resistance: The Warsaw Ghetto Uprising*. Houghton Mifflin/ United States Holocaust Memorial Museum. 1994. 277 pages. (S)

Written by the director of the research center at Yad Vashem and a survivor of the Warsaw Ghetto uprising and the concentration camps, this book provides a comprehensive examination of the uprising. Photos and excerpts from documents, including letters and diaries, are here. This book is an excellent resource for adults or for advanced secondary students doing more in-depth reading on the uprising.

Lawless, Charles. . . . *and God Cried: The Holocaust Remembered*. Wieser & Wieser, 1994. 175 pages. (S)

Lawless juxtaposes powerful photographs with a compelling narrative that chronicles the times of the Third Reich and its systematic attempt to destroy European Jews, Gypsies, homosexuals, and political opponents. He presents major figures, victims, persecutors, and rescuers and shows their roles during this time.

Rashke, Richard. *Escape from Sobibor*. Houghton Mifflin, 1982. 389 pages. (S)

Rashke interviewed thirty survivors to describe life in the camp at Sobibor in eastern Poland, one of the deadliest of the concentration camps. It was also the site of the most significant rebellion against Nazi guards. The Nazis destroyed most of the records of this camp and little has been known about the 600 Jews who revolted until now.

Steiner, Jean-François. *Treblinka.* Simon & Schuster, 1967; New American Library, 1979; A Meridian Book, 1994. Originally published in French. 415 pages. (S)

Awarded the Merit of Educational Distinction by the International Center for Holocaust Studies of the Anti-Defamation League, this book is appropriate for adults or for advanced secondary school students seeking to do more in-depth research. Treblinka was a death camp established to kill as many people as fast as possible. After the revolt by its prisoners, the camp was razed and all its documents destroyed. Steiner provides an overall picture of the camp as a world of its own based on personal interviews with survivors and testimony gathered by the Polish Court of Inquiry in 1945 and later by the Yad Vashem Institute.

Yahil, Leni. *The Holocaust: The Fate of European Jewry, 1932–1945.* Translated from the Hebrew by Ina Friedman and Haya Galai. Oxford University Press, 1987. 808 pages. (S)

Yahil's examination of the Holocaust is divided into three major time periods. Part I describes events from 1932 until Hitler's takeover in 1939; Part II covers the beginning of the war until 1941; and Part III examines the preparations in 1941 for the attack on Russia to the end of the war in 1945. This book is a signifcant and major work in Holocaust studies and as such, is a valuable resource for adults. It is also appropriate for advanced secondary students seeking more in-depth information about the Holocaust.

Literature Involvement:
Suggestions and Issues for Responding
and Thinking

Learning about the Holocaust is often a powerful experience for young people. They need opportunities to reflect upon what they are learning and to express their feelings. They also need opportunities to clarify misconceptions and to seek additional information. The following suggestions can be selected according to their appropriateness for the various age groups and then used to provide these opportunities.

- Compare what you have learned about the Holocaust with what you thought you already knew about it. What new information did you learn? What did you learn that surprised you? What else do you want to know?

- Select a quote that had a significant impact on you from one of the books you read. Discuss its significance for you. (In a classroom setting, students can write their quotes on the chalkboard or on paper strips to display on the walls. These quotes then can be used to prompt group discussion and as a springboard for writing.)

- Examine the photographs in the books and others that tell the story of the Holocaust. Select from five to seven photos that make the biggest impression on you and describe why.

- Select one of the events that occurred during the period 1933–1945 that seems especially important to you. Learn more about it and then present that information to your classmates.

- Imagine you are a newspaper journalist. Select any of the following topics to write a front page article for your paper: 1) The Rise of Hitler; 2) Life in the Third Reich; 3) Nazi Actions Against the Jews; 4) Conditions in the Concentration Camps.

- Imagine you are a television news correspondent. Prepare and deliver a news report on any of the following: 1) German invasion of (select a country); 2) *Kristallnacht*; 3) The Warsaw Ghetto uprising; 4) Liberation from Auschwitz (or one of the other camps).

- We often think of the Holocaust in terms of the systematic destruction of the Jews, but they were not the only group persecuted. Select one of the other groups and research why they were included and their treatment.

- Hitler persecuted people based on their religious and cultural heritage. What does it mean to have freedom of religion? What freedoms are we guaranteed by our Bill of Rights? Why were European Jews denied their legal and constitutional protection for the period 1933–1945.

- In order to understand the magnitude of the Holocaust we need to look at the structure of the camps. Select one camp, such as Auschwitz. Do research to determine the following: 1) What was the nature of the camp (transient camp, death camp, or forced labor camp)? 2) How large was it in area? 3) How long was the camp open (dates)? 4) How many guards worked there? 5) Who was the commandant and what happened to him or her? 6) Who were the prisoners (were they Jews or Gypsies or communists or other political prisoners, or was there a mixture of groups)? 7) How many prisoners were sent there (estimations) and how many survived? Compile your findings as a data sheet.

- Role play an experience you have had with scapegoating, prejudice, or discrimination. What did you learn from these experiences? What can we do to help eliminate these kinds of actions and behaviors?

- The Wall of Remembrance in the United States Holocaust Memorial Museum has more than 3,000 tiles handpainted by young people as a memorial to children who died during the Holocaust. Design and paint a tile expressing your reaction to one of the significant events that occurred during the Holocaust.

- Write an informational book about some aspect of the Holocaust for someone with little or no background knowledge of it. Include why it is important to learn about the Holocaust.

- Express in a creative format something significant that you have learned about the Holocaust. Examples of types of creative expression include the visual arts, music, creative dramatics, dance, poetry, or other forms of writing.

3

They Were There

Personal Narratives, Biographies, Autobiographies, Poetry

To the people who say there was no Holocaust, tell them I
was there. I'm real. It happened.

Erwin Baum, survivor of Auschwitz, from
We Remember the Holocaust

This chapter presents books that tell the stories of young people
and others who actually lived during the Holocaust and were involved directly in it one way or another. These books are autobiographical or biographical in nature, with the authors describing
either their own experiences or those of others. Many are personal
narratives of survivors, individuals who beat the odds by courage,
tenacity, and often quirks of fate. Some are stories of surviving in
the camps, while others are of resistance or hiding, but all are stories of bravery. The killing of Jews was so pervasive and capricious
that survival became a daily act of courage and of faith. Not all of
the individuals whose stories are told here did survive. For example,
we have included several selections about both Anne Frank and
Hannah Senesh. Their courage and dedication make their life stories gripping and inspiring, yet poignant.

The magnitude of what happened to those who lived and those
whose lives were taken during the Holocaust has mandated that the

survivors bear witness to their experiences. These accounts forge a human connection between author and reader. These narratives encourage youthful readers to make personal commitments as they try to understand about the times. In addition to biographies, autographies, and personal narratives, this chapter contains information about poetry and artists' works. Suggestions for using the books described in this chapter are also provided.

Prior to Reading: Think About . . .

Biographies and personal narratives usually have a powerful impact on the reader. They can help to personalize historical events and to put a real face on what otherwise might seem to be just a dry—or in the case of the Holocaust, overwhelming—collection of facts and statistics. It is important to help young people put these stories about real people into an historical context and to make a connection between the lives they are reading about and their own lives. The following questions can be used to prompt this discussion:

- Do you know anyone who lived during the Holocaust? Have you ever read about someone from that time? Or seen a film or a video about someone? What do you remember about that person(s)?

- Imagine that life in your community changes. A powerful political leader begins to persecute members of your family and friends and associates. Your family decides that it must flee. What would it be like to select only a few of your belongings and leave, knowing that you would probably never return to your home, friends, and possessions?

- What would it be like not to know where you were going, how you would get there, and what it would be like when you did—if you made it?

- Have you ever experienced a time you were terribly frightened and felt unsafe? What made you feel safe again?

- Before reading any of the personal narratives, biographies, or autobiographies recommended in this chapter, brainstorm a list of people whom you consider to be heroes. Then create a list of characteristics that are heroic. Share your lists with other students in your group or class. How are your lists the same or different?

- What do you think life was like for someone your age during the Holocaust? In what ways do you think it was the same? How do you think it was different?

- Read the quotes listed with the book you have chosen (or that will be read to you.) What do you think they mean? What do you think they reveal about the people and the times?

Focus: They Were There

Alicia, My Story by Alicia Appleman-Jurman. (S, JM)

Anne Frank, Beyond the Diary: A Photographic Remembrance by Ruud van der Rol and Rian Verhoeven. (JM, E)

Assignment: Rescue, An Autobiography by Varian Fry. (S, JM)

The Big Lie: A True Story by Isabella Leitner with Irving A. Leitner. (E, JM, P)

The Cage by Ruth Minsky Sender. (JM)

Children of the Resistance by Lore Cowan. (S, JM)

Clara's Story by Clara Isaacman, as told to Joan Adess Grossman. (JM, S)

Elie Wiesel: Messenger from the Holocaust by Carol Greene. (AL)

Father of the Orphans: The Story of Janusz Korczak by Mark Bernheim. (S, JM)

Hiding to Survive: Stories of Jewish Children Rescued from the Holocaust by Maxine B. Rosenberg. (JM, S, E)

Hilde and Eli: Children of the Holocaust by David A. Adler. Illustrated by Karen Ritz. (P, E)

I Am a Star: Child of the Holocaust by Inge Auerbacher. (JM, E, S)

In Kindling Flame: The Story of Hannah Senesh, 1921–1944 by Linda Atkinson. (S, JM)

Night by Elie Wiesel. (S)

A Picture Book of Anne Frank by David A. Adler. Illustrated by Karen Ritz. (P, E)

Raoul Wallenberg by Michael Nicholson and David Winner. (E, JM)

Rescue: The Story of How Gentiles Saved Jews in the Holocaust by Milton Meltzer. (JM, S)

Rescuers: Portraits of Moral Courage in the Holocaust by Gay Block and Malka Drucker. (S, JM)

So Young to Die: The Story of Hannah Senesh by Candice F. Ransom. (E, JM)

Struggle by Sara Zyskind. (S, JM)

The Survivor in Us All: Four Young Sisters in the Holocaust by Erna F. Rubinstein. (JM, S)

Upon the Head of a Goat: A Childhood in Hungary, 1939–44 by Aranka Siegal. (JM, S)

The Upstairs Room by Johanna Reiss. (JM, E)

All School Levels

Greene, Carol. *Elie Wiesel: Messenger from the Holocaust.* Children's Press, 1987, 32 pages.

"I owe something to the dead," he said. . . . "Anyone who does not remember betrays them again." (p. 29)

At a Glance ▪ This book is a brief account of Elie Wiesel's experiences during the Holocaust. While it could be read to and understood by younger readers, it is appropriate for all ages as an introduction to this important man. The book also includes Wiesel's Nobel Peace Prize acceptance speech, which is appropriate for older and more sophisticated readers.

Summary ▪ This short pictorial selection describes a number of Elie Wiesel's experiences in concentration camps. The book provides readers with appropriate factual information about the horrors of the times; however, the description of Wiesel's experiences puts a human face on the tragedy. Elie Wiesel received the 1986 Nobel Peace Prize for his role in informing the world about social, political, and religious inequities.

> Sometimes we must interfere. When human lives are endangered, when human dignity is in jeopardy, national borders and sensitivities become irrelevant. Where ever men or women are persecuted because of their race, religion or political views, that place must—at that moment—become the center of the universe. (p. 30, Wiesel's Nobel Peace Prize acceptance speech).

Teaching Considerations ▪ Wiesel has played a significant role in informing the world of the realities of the Holocaust. Older or more advanced students can do research to get a perspective of the impact that he has had. Greene's book provides an appropriate introduction for secondary school students to Wiesel's book, *Night*, described in this chapter. The film/video, *Holocaust: Liberation of Auschwitz,* has the potential to enhance the understanding of mature students of the conditions in Auschwitz (see chapter 7). For younger readers, *The Big Lie: A True Story* by Isabella Leitner is an appropriate follow-up book.

Primary School Level

Adler, David A. Illustrated by Karen Ritz. *Hilde and Eli: Children of the Holocaust.* Holiday House, 1994. 30 pages.

It seemed to Hilde that JEWS NOT WANTED signs were being posted everywhere. She felt scared and unwelcome in her own country. (unnumbered)

At a Glance ▪ This picture book tells the parallel stories of two real children who died during the Holocaust. While it can be read aloud to primary school children, its use should be limited to those with background already about the Holocaust who are prepared for the frightening nature of the death of the children. This book can be used to increase the children's understanding of the consequences of Nazi action.

Summary ▪ The first half of this picture book tells the story of Hilde Rosenzweig and her family. Hilde was born in the city of Frankfurt am Main, Germany, in 1923. Her family owned a linen store and lived in an apartment. Her childhood is described against the backdrop of the political changes occuring in Germany. Hilde and her mother died when the freight car in which they were being taken to a ghetto in Latvia was filled with poisonous gas by the SS. The second half of the picture book tells the story of Eli Lax and his family who lived in a small village in the Carpathian Mountains in Czechoslovakia. Born in 1932, he was the youngest of six children. His father was a rabbi and a teacher. Eli liked to play outdoors, but he also was a good student. Then the Nazis invaded his country and life changed dramatically. Eventually Eli, his father, and his brother were killed in the gas chambers of Auschwitz. Although the two children never knew each other, they and their families were persecuted and suffered simply because they were Jewish.

> Eli's father considered escaping with his children, but there was no place to go. (unnumbered)

Teaching Considerations ▪ This moving and powerful picture book should be used with great sensitivity with young children. The colored illustrations effectively enhance the story of what happened to Hilde, Eli, and their families. Primary school children could be introduced to the Holocaust with one of Adler's other books, *The Number on My Grandfather's Arm* (see chapter 2). Eve Bunting's *The Terrible Things* is appropriate to use with both primary and elementary school children (see chapter 6). Children will need ample opportunities to share their feelings about what happens in this book through discussion, art activities, and creative dramatics. For elementary school-age children, this book can be paired with books that provide more detail about the Holocaust such as Seymour Rossel's *The Holocaust: The Fire That Raged*, in chapter 2.

Adler, David A. Illustrated by Karen Ritz.
A Picture Book of Anne Frank.
Holiday House, 1993. 29 pages.

"Memories mean more to me than dresses," Anne wrote later. (unnumbered)

At a Glance ▪ This beautifully illustrated picture book tells the story of Anne Frank in a simple and poignant manner. It is appropriate to be read to primary school children; elementary school children could read it for themselves as an introduction to Anne Frank.

Summary ▪ Anne Frank was born in Germany where her family had lived for hundreds of years. With the rise of Hitler and Nazism, her family moved to Amsterdam. They lived there safely until the invasion by the German Army. As conditions became worse, the family went into hiding with four other people shortly after Anne's thirteenth birthday. In hiding for more than two years, Anne recorded her experiences and feelings in her diary. Discovered by the Nazis, they were sent to the camps. Anne and her sister, Margot, died shortly before the camps were liberated.

> After eighteen months in the hideaway, Anne wrote, "I am longing, so longing for everything . . . to talk, for freedom, for friends, to be alone. And I do so long . . . to cry!" (unnumbered)

Teaching Considerations ▪ Anne Frank's life is a moving story that provides students with opportunities to personalize the Holocaust. Help your students to identify with Anne, her experiences, and her feelings by imagining how they would have spent their time in the annex. The illustrations in this account of Anne's life are hauntingly effective. Give children ample opportunities to look at them and discuss them. This picture book biography of Anne Frank is a good introduction to two other biographies not included in this book: *Anne Frank: Life in Hiding* by Johanna Hurwitz and *Anne Frank, 1929–1945*, of the *LifeTimes* Series by Richard Tames. Ruud van der Rol and Rian Verhoeven's book, *Anne Frank, Beyond the Diary: A Photographic Remembrance* is also appropriate for elementary school children. It is discussed in this chapter.

Additional Titles: Primary School Level

The Big Lie: A True Story by Isabella Leitner with Irving A. Leitner. (E)

Elie Wiesel: Messenger from the Holocaust by Carol Greene. (AL)

Elementary School Level

**Leitner, Isabella, with Irving A. Leitner. *The Big Lie: A True Story.*
Scholastic, 1992. 79 pages.**

> As the days passed, we learned what Auschwitz was. It
> was a huge Nazi death camp surrounded by barbed wire
> fences. . . . At Auschwitz, between ten and twenty thou-
> sand people were killed every day in the summer of
> 1944. (p. 46)

At a Glance ▪ Isabella Leitner describes her experiences and those
of her family when they are sent to Auschwitz in 1944. This book
is appropriate for elementary school students and some students at
junior high/middle school level. It also can be read aloud to primary
school children.

Summary ▪ Isabella Leitner, her parents, four sisters, and a brother
lived in a small town in Hungary. In 1939 after gangs terrorized
the local Jews, her father went to America to try to arrange for
immigration papers for the family. World War II and the Nazis still
seemed far away until March 20, 1944, when the Germans invaded
Budapest. Overnight life changed as special orders were announced
restricting the rights of Jews. In May, her family and all the other
Jewish families in the town were deported to the Auschwitz death
camp in Poland. Separated from their mother and youngest sister,
the others managed to survive and eventually were sent to other
camps. During a forced march, Isabella and two of her sisters escaped and hid in a dog house until they were liberated by the Red
Army.

> "We have a father in America. We want to join him. We
> were in Auschwitz. We lost our mother and two sisters.
> We lost our brother. We want to go to America." (p. 71)

Teaching Considerations ▪ This is a powerful story of loss. It will
evoke a strong emotional response in readers. Provide students with
opportunities to examine their responses through class discussions,
dramatizations, and/or media expressions. Some students may
want to learn more about Isabella Leitner and read her other books.
Other appropriate follow-up books are Radsom's *So Young to Die:
The Story of Hannah Senesh* for elementary school students and

Siegal's *Upon the Head of a Goat: A Childhood in Hungary, 1939–44* for junior high/middle school students (see entries in this chapter).

Nicholson, Michael, and David Winner. *Raoul Wallenberg.* Gareth Stevens, 1989; Morehouse Publishing, 1990. 68 pages. (E, JM)

> Raoul Wallenberg had been sent by his government, but he was armed with little more than courage and his extraordinary personality. (p. 5)

At a Glance ▪ This is the story of a true hero, Raoul Wallenberg, the Swedish diplomat, who saved the lives of 100,000 Hungarian Jews. It could be read aloud to elementary school students. It is also appropriate for junior high/middle school students.

Summary ▪ As World War II was coming to an end, the Nazis made one last major effort to destroy European Jews, this time in Hungary. In 1944, the United States and Sweden cooperated to help save Jews from the death camps. They sent an American-educated Swedish diplomat named Raoul Wallenberg to Budapest. Wallenberg matched wits with Nazi leaders and saved many lives. He invented *Schutz-passes*, which looked like passports, but had no legal status. Jews with these papers convinced the Nazis that they were protected by the Swedish government. When the Russians entered Hungary, Wallenberg disappeared. His fate at the hands of the Russians has been the source of speculation for many years.

> He should have been treated as a great hero. Yet, to the new rulers of Budapest, the Soviets, he seemed to be a criminal. (p. 51)

Teaching Considerations ▪ Many students have a media-influenced perspective about heroism. Work with students to develop an understanding that courage and heroism are the result of ordinary people acting honorably in difficult situations without concern for their own well-being. Rittner and Myers's book, *The Courage to Care: Rescuers of Jews During the Holocaust,* is a good follow-up book. Junior high/middle school students can compare Nicholson and Winner's book on Wallenberg with one by Sharon Linnea, *Raoul Wallenberg: The Man Who Stopped Death* (see entry in this chapter). The video/film, *Raoul Wallenberg: Between the Lines*, can be screened for its appropriateness for this age level (see chapter 7).

Ransom, Candice F. *So Young to Die: The Story of Hannah Senesh.* Scholastic, 1993. 152 pages.

> The new term was only a few weeks old when Hannah confronted anti-Semitism head-on. The incident revolved around her position as an officer in the Literary Society. (p. 26).

At a Glance ▪ Candice Ransom recreates the life of a young Hungarian, Hannah Senesh, who immigrated to Palestine in 1939 when she was only eighteen. Four years later she returned to Hungary as part of a special mission to fight the Nazis. This book is appropriate for elementary school students and some readers at the junior high/ middle school level. It also is a good book to read aloud.

Summary ▪ Hannah Senesh loved to write poetry and as a youth dreamed of becoming a writer. Her father, who died when she was only six, had been a well-known and highly respected Hungarian author. She grew up in a privileged environment in which she was one of the few Jews who attended a Protestant girls' school with high academic standards. Hannah did very well there in spite of growing antagonism against Jews in her own country of Hungary and in Europe in general. She won prizes and recognition and was considered to be the finest student in the school. Although her family had not actively practiced their faith, the rise of the Nazis and changing conditions in Hungary had an impact on Hannah. She became a Zionist and dreamed of going to Palestine and working to establish a Jewish homeland. She fulfilled her dream shortly after she graduated from high school. She worked in a Kibbutz and made Palestine her home, but was concerned about worsening conditions back in Hungary. Hannah became a member of a secret group working with the British Air Force to return to Hungary to rescue Allied pilots and Jews. She parachuted behind enemy lines and returned to her native country where she was captured by the Nazis. She was put in prison, but she never faltered in her beliefs or her courage. She was twenty-three when she was executed.

The book has photographs, an epilogue about the tributes to Hannah, a section entitled "What Happened to the People in Hannah Senesh's Life," a bibliography, and an index. All of these sections are both informative and interesting.

> Hannah Senesh converted prisoners to Zionism, even as they waited on benches outside the Nazi offices. She began to feel fulfilled once more. Her purpose in life was to give people hope, even in this terrible place. (p. 120)

Teaching Considerations ▪ As students read this book they will become aware of the inequities that Hannah faced in school. Discuss discrimination and its impact with your students. Give them opportunities to talk about discrimination they have experienced or examples that they are aware of with other people. Students who are interested in Hannah Senesh will want to read her poetry and other books about her. See the other entries in this chapter.

Additional Titles: Elementary School Level

Anne Frank, Beyond the Diary: A Photographic Remembrance by Ruud van der Rol and Rian Verhoeven. (JM)

Elie Wiesel: Messenger from the Holocaust by Carol Greene. (AL)

Hiding to Survive: Stories of Jewish Children Rescued from the Holocaust by Maxine B. Rosenberg. (JM)

Hilde and Eli: Children of the Holocaust by David A. Adler. Illustrated by Karen Ritz. (P)

I Am a Star: Child of the Holocaust by Inge Auerbacher. (JM)

A Picture Book of Anne Frank by David A. Adler. Illustrated by Karen Ritz. (P)

The Upstairs Room by Johanna Reiss. (JM)

Junior High/Middle School Level

Auerbacher, Inge. *I Am a Star: Child of the Holocaust.* **Prentice-Hall, 1986, Puffin Books, 1993. 87 pages.**

Of fifteen thousand children imprisoned in the Terezin concentration camp in Czechoslovakia between 1941 and 1945, about one hundred survived. I am one of them. (p. 1)

At a Glance ▪ Inge Auerbacher's personal narrative is interspersed with photographs, drawings, and poetry recalling her childhood experiences from ages seven to ten in Terezin concentration camp in Czechoslovakia, 1942–1945. While the reading level of this book is appropriate for junior high/middle school students, it is powerful enough to appeal to older readers and some elementary school readers as well as to both genders.

Summary ▪ Inge Auerbacher, her parents, and grandparents lived happy, peaceful lives in southern Germany. Her father's family had been in Germany for 200 years and he was decorated with the Iron Cross for bravery in the service of his country during World War I. Their lives are changed dramatically as one decree after another deprives Jews of their rights. When Inge is seven, she and her parents are sent to a concentration camp in Czechoslovakia. Terezin is a transit camp where people are held and then selected to be sent to the extermination camps. For three years, Inge and her parents survive the horrors of the camp until their liberation by the Allies.

> One small candle emitted a ray of light,
> A beacon of hope against this darkest night.
> (from the poem, "Liberation," p. 68)

Teaching Considerations ▪ Provide the readers with ample time to examine the drawings and reflect upon the poetry. For some, these will serve as a springboard for creating their own drawings and poetry expressing their feelings about what they are learning. An effective prompt for discussion of *I Am a Star* is to have students talk about what their lives were like between the ages of seven and ten. Have them compare and contrast their lives with that of Inge.

Isaacman, Clara, as told to Joan Adess Grossman. *Clara's Story.* Jewish Publication Society of America, 1984. 120 pages.

> This is like a bad dream, I thought. The walking, the horse, the bombing, people screaming and running, the suddenly dead bodies all seemed too strange and horrible to be real. Is this really happening to me? (p. 28)

At a Glance ▪ Clara Heller Isaacman describes her experiences and those of her family as they struggled to survive during the Nazi occupation of Belgium. Well-written and exciting, this book is appropriate for both junior high/middle school students and secondary students; it will appeal to readers of both genders.

Summary ▪ On the eve of World War II, Clara Heller and her family lived in Antwerp, Belgium. Her family moved there from Romania when her father, on his way to vote, was beaten because he was a Jew. In Belgium, the family enjoyed religious freedom and were prosperous members of the community. Clara was a happy, active teenager, but her life changed dramatically when the Germans invaded Belgium. Her family attempted to flee, first to France, and then to England, but to no avail. Conditions deteriorated as the Jews were systematically deprived of their basic rights and freedoms. Her family, helped by the Resistance, had to go into hiding, moving from one place to another for two and one-half years. Although her father and brother died, Clara and the rest of the family survived relentless dangers, hardships, tedium, and betrayal while also helping others to survive.

> Dear Daddy, dear Heshie, I thought, dear friends and neighbors whom I have lost. I will try to make my life worthy of your memory. You will always be with me. I felt a faint, warm breeze and, for the first time in many months, took a deep, full . . . free . . . breath of air. (p. 119)

Teaching Considerations ▪ *Clara's Story* lends itself well to discussing how people change as a result of adversity in their lives. Students can be helped to see how some people are able to meet the challenges of adversity, while others are not. Have them identify with this concept by describing changes they have experienced in their lives as a result of adversity. They can also compare their daily lives with Clara's at the same age. Rosenberg's *Hiding to Survive: Stories of Jewish Children Rescued from the Holocaust* and Cowan's *Children of the Resistance* can be used as follow-up books (see entries in this chapter).

Meltzer, Milton. Rescue: The Story of How Gentiles Saved Jews in the Holocaust.
HarperCollins, 1988. 168 pages.

"The Holocaust" is the term Jews themselves chose to describe what happened to them during World War II.

The term is related to the word *olah* in the Hebrew Bible. Its religious meaning is 'Burnt Sacrifice.' Over the 3500-year span of Jewish history, the Holocaust was the most massive catastrophe. Six million died, two out of every three Jews in Europe, one third of the world's Jews. But don't think of them as millions. Do that and you miss the truth of the murder of each individual man, woman, and child. (p. 2)

At a Glance ▪ This book tells the stories of Gentiles who risked imprisonment and even death to help Jews to escape the Nazis. It is appropriate for junior high/middle school and secondary school readers and will hold the attention of readers of both genders.

Summary ▪ Milton Meltzer presents the stories of those non-Jewish individuals who earned the title "Righteous Gentiles" for their acts of humanity. While this book provides stories of many well-known individuals, such as Raoul Wallenberg, King Christian X of Denmark, Oskar Schindler, and others, it also provides glimpses of numerous ordinary people who made a difference by saving Jews. This book provides a partial answer to the haunting question: "How could people stand by and let the Nazis slaughter millions of Jews?" There were those who did not stand by, but who took courageous stands.

They [Righteous Gentiles] are, all of them, human spirits whose lives witness the truth that there is an alternative to the passive acceptance of evil. Where they lived, goodness happened.

And where we live, goodness can happen. (p.159)

Teaching Considerations ▪ Collect other resources about these "Righteous Gentiles." Let students select one of the Righteous Gentiles and explore more about his or her role in the Holocaust. Have them look at the risks the the person took and examples of courage. Provide opportunities for the class members to share their findings. Appropriate companion books are *A Place to Hide: True Stories of Holocaust Rescues* by Jayne Pettit and *The Courage to Care: Rescuers of Jews During the Holocaust* edited by Rittner and Myers, in this chapter. *The Courage to Care* is also available as a film/video (see chapter 7). Some students may want to read Corrie ten Boom's

The Hiding Place or *The Upstairs Room* by Johanna Reiss, also in this chapter.

Reiss, Johanna. *The Upstairs Room.*
Thomas Y. Crowell, 1972; Harper Keypoint, 1987. 179 pages.

> The next week the Germans moved in. At the same time Sini and I started to live in bed. October 17, 1944—that's what the calendar said. The days were long and silent. Evenings were just as long and silent. Sini hardly talked. Maybe she would if I made her mad enough, but how could we fight if we could only whisper? (pp. 145–46)

At a Glance ▪ Johanna Reiss tells of her personal experiences at the age of ten, as she (Annie de Leeuw) and her sister, Sini, are sent away from the rest of their family into hiding as the Germans occupy Holland. Among the awards this book has received are the Newbery Honor Book, Jane Addams Peace Association Honor Book, and the Jewish Book Council Juvenile Book Award. It is appropriate for junior high/middle school readers and some elementary school readers.

Summary ▪ For many Jewish families in Holland, the only escape after the Nazi occupation was to go into hiding with the help of Gentiles who opposed the Nazis. The Oostervelds didn't know the deLeeuw family, but they opened their home for the two young girls, Annie and Sini, and hid them upstairs in their rural farmhouse for over two years. Briefly, Nazi soldiers also stayed at the farm, using it as a headquarters. During that period the sisters spent most of their time silently in bed to avoid detection. The relationship between the girls and the Oostervelds, Johan and Dientje, and Johan's mother, Opoe, was a warm and loving one. When the war ended Annie and Sini and the Oostervelds were all reluctant to have the sisters leave.

> I took my girls upstairs to the front room. Johan left the hiding place intact. "That's the place Mommy used to crawl into," I said. "See whether you can do it now," they asked me. Obediently I went over to the closet and got on the floor. That's as far as I got. "Look, she's crying," my girls said. (p. 24)

Teaching Considerations ▪ Have your students imagine that they are either Annie or Sini in *The Upstairs Room* and describe a typical day. Then ask them to select a part of their day and act it out as a scene with another person. *Hide and Seek* by Ida Vos is a good companion book (see chapter 4). These books can be used to introduce Meltzer's book, *Rescue: The Story of How Gentiles Saved Jews in the Holocaust,* in this chapter. Reiss has another book, *The Journey Back,* that describes her experiences after the war, described here in chapter 6.

Rosenberg, Maxine B. *Hiding to Survive: Stories of Jewish Children Rescued from the Holocaust.* Clarion Books, 1994. 166 pages.

The hayloft was very long and low, so we couldn't stand up in it. During the day we mostly lay in the straw, but at night we crawled into a tiny thatch shelter that Mr. Plotowski had partitioned off from the rest of the area. (Sylvia Richter, p. 74)

At a Glance ▪ Rosenberg has collected the first-person accounts of fourteen people who spent the war years in hiding, protected by ordinary people against the Nazis. This book is appropriate for junior high/middle school students and some secondary school students. The first-person accounts are effective to read aloud to elementary students.

Summary ▪ Often we think of victims of the Holocaust as those who ended up in concentrations camps throughout Europe. This book tells the story of other victims, those who spent part of their childhoods hidden in barns, attics, chimneys, chicken coops, or even pretending to be part of the Christian families that sheltered them from the Nazis. Fourteen survivors, who spent their war years in hiding, relate their stories of fear and danger while also relating the acts of courage of those who helped these young people. Each entry includes photographs of the survivors, one from their childhood and the other taken as an adult.

Meanwhile I was masquerading as a Polish Christian. Yet I was always terrified. Every time I walked down the street, there were Germans mingling with the crowd. (Aviva Blumberg, p. 110)

Teaching Considerations ▪ These narratives provide a vivid image of survival. Help your students to recognize the power of telling a story by looking at narratives. Ask them to create a narrative account, imagining that they are in hiding. Companion books for junior high/middle school students are *The Upstairs Room* by Johanna Reiss and any of the books by or about Anne Frank; older readers may want to look for *Rescuers: Portraits of Moral Courage in the Holocaust* by Block and Drucker, all in this chapter.

Rubinstein, Erna F. *The Survivor in Us All: Four Young Sisters in the Holocaust.* Original title, *The Survivor in Us All: A Memoir of the Holocaust.* Archon Books, 1983. 185 pages. (JM, S)

> We certainly came out of Auschwitz. And yet there was a burning wound inside of us that was Auschwitz. It burned constantly like the flame that had consumed the bodies of our beloved mother . . . many, many relatives and friends . . . We had lost our dignity in Auschwitz . . . Even more than all that, we had learned to live with death, and the strong drive for survival penetrated all of us. (p. 152)

At a Glance ▪ Told from the perspective of a teenage girl, this book captures not only the horrors of the Holocaust for a Polish Jewish family, but also their courage and determination to stay together. It is appropriate for junior high/middle school and secondary school readers.

Summary ▪ The author, who is "Ruth" in the book, tells the story of her Polish Jewish family from September, 1939 to May, 1945. When the Germans invaded Poland, her family, amidst general confusion and uncertainty, decided to flee their small town to join their grandparents in Krakow where they thought they would be safe. They were forced to move into the ghetto where they had to work as laborers to survive. The book details their struggles as conditions steadily worsened. Finally the family members were sent to various concentration camps. Only Ruth and her sisters survived by escaping during the "Death March" out of Auschwitz.

> I became very gloomy at times, and then it was one or another of my sisters who had a spark of hope, and al-

ways carried it to all four of us. It was enough for one
to say something good, and we all responded to it . . .
(p. 166)

Teaching Considerations ▪ Have the students discuss what they
think the title, *The Survivor in Us All*, means and what the implications might be for their own lives. Help them to identify the characteristics of the four sisters, their similarities and differences, and
how they responded to various situations. Guide the students to see
the strength the sisters developed from their commitment to each
other and how it helped them to survive. *The Cage* by Ruth Minsky
Sender and *Alicia, My Story* by Alicia Appleman-Jurman, in this
chapter, can be used as companion books. Films/videos that could
be shown are *Images Before My Eyes* and *The Last Chapter*, in
chapter 7.

Sender, Ruth Minsky. *The Cage*.
Macmillan, 1986. 245 pages.

I hear Mama's voice, filled with hope. A world full of
people will not be silent. We will not perish in vain. She
was so sure. But she perished, and the world was silent.
(p. 4)

At a Glance ▪ Sender relates her experiences from the last days before the Nazi occupation in 1939 to the Russian liberation of the
camp at Grafenort where she was confined. This book could be
used as either an alternative to *The Diary of Anne Frank* or as a
supplement to it in a junior high/middle school class.

Summary ▪ The Nazi occupation of Poland caused hardship for all
Jews. In Lodz, the Minsky family suffered as did their friends, but
for teenager Riva (Ruth) the situation worsened when her mother
was taken away by the Nazis. Then it was her responsibility to keep
her family of three younger brothers together. They had to try to
survive in the Lodz Ghetto where they faced numerous obstacles,
including the illness of their youngest brother. They protected him
from the Nazis until he died. As conditions worsened in the ghetto,
Riva and her brothers volunteered to be transported to a "work
camp" in the hopes that they would be able to stay together. As
soon as they arrived at Auschwitz, they were separated and Riva
never saw her brothers again. While life in the ghetto had been

difficult, every day at Auschwitz was a struggle for survival. Riva's life improved after she was transferred to a work camp at Mittelsteine, where although the work was grueling, the immediate threat of death was reduced. Riva is a poet and her gift helped her to survive when the woman who was the camp commandant supported her talent for writing.

> I pick up the notebook with shaking hands. This did not really happen. I must be dreaming. There is something human in that woman, something that can be moved by a poem. I touch the small notebook. It is real. I am not dreaming. It is real. It is real. (p. 217)

Teaching Considerations ▪ In *The Cage*, Riva writes poetry and it helps her to survive. Have your students write a poem about a difficult time in their lives. The documentaries *Lodz Ghetto* as well as *Images Before My Eyes* or the historical film *The Last Chapter* can be shown to provide them with more background on Jewish life in Poland. Sender has also written *The Holocaust Lady* and *To Life* (in chapter 6).

Siegal, Aranka. *Upon the Head of a Goat:*
A Childhood in Hungary 1939–44.
Farrar, Straus & Giroux, 1981; Puffin Books, 1994. 215 pages.

> In the fall, a few days before school was to open, we heard that Jewish children would no longer be permitted to attend the public schools. (p. 101)

At a Glance ▪ Aranka Siegal relates her own experiences growing up in Hungary during World War II from 1939 when she was nine years old until 1944 when she and her family are taken to Auschwitz. While this book is appropriate for junior high/middle school readers, the excitement and danger in it make it interesting for a wide range of readers.

Summary ▪ This Newbery Honor Book is a riveting story of one family's efforts to survive as war and the persecution of Jews moved ever closer to their lives. Piri (Aranka Siegal) grows from the age of nine to almost fifteen in the book. Nine-year-old Piri's life was changed when her visit to her grandmother was extended to a year-long stay because the German soldiers closed the border with her native Hungary. Even after she returned home to Beregszasz, she realized that things were not as they used to be. There was a distance between her and her two closest friends because Piri was Jewish and her friends were not. Her mother, a strong and resourceful woman, managed to keep her family together and to provide for them in spite of the difficult times. They faced food shortages, imprisonment in the ghetto, and finally they were loaded on a train headed for Auschwitz.

> "We are all God's children," Babi used to say, meaning
> both Jews and Christians. Did she mean Germans, too?
> I wish that I had her to ask. They did not look like anybody's children, and they looked not at us, but through
> us as if we didn't exist. (p. 211)

Teaching Considerations ▪ Help your students to identify with Piri's experiences when she is made to feel that she is an outsider even with her friends. Have them focus on the idea of belonging, and how they can help others to be included and never feel that they are outsiders. Students may want to read the sequel, *Grace in the Wilderness: After the Liberation 1945–48* (see chapter 6).

van der Rol, Ruud, and Rian Verhoeven. *Anne Frank, Beyond the Diary: A Photographic Remembrance.* Viking Press, 1993. 113 pages.

> As we grew, and as the legend grew as well, Anne
> Frank had in some essential way ceased to be an ordinary person. These pictures make her whole again: one
> little Jewish girl, one life growing, thriving, struggling to
> break the surface of its soil like a seedling just at the
> time that the soil was poisoned. The failed flowering
> means more with the seeds. Seeing the baby Anne, the
> smiling Anne, the free Anne, makes her life all that much
> more ordinary. And that much more heroic and heartbreaking. (Anna Quindlen, p. xii)

At a Glance ▪ This award-winning book would be an excellent complement to *The Diary of Anne Frank*. It provides interesting background that could be read by or to both junior high/middle school students and elementary students.

Summary ▪ Anne Frank is arguably the best known victim of the Holocaust. She has become a symbol for the murder of millions of innocent people. In this book the history of the family is told with a complement of photographs. The book combines Frank family photographs, historical photographs, excerpts from the diary, photographs of diary pages, and maps along with an accounting of the times.

> Margot died in March 1945. A few days later, Anne died as well. The camp was liberated by British soldiers a few weeks later in April.
>
> Otto Frank was the only one of the group from the Secret Annex to survive the war. He was still in Auschwitz when the Russians liberated the camp on January 27, 1945. (pp. 101–02)

Teaching Considerations ▪ This book can be used as an accompaniment to the *Diary*. Her *Diary* is frequently included in literature anthologies for junior high/middle school students. Have students discuss how the information in this book affects their reading of it. Films, videos and audio recordings are also available (see chapter 7). Other books related to Anne Frank are described in this chapter as well as a play in chapter 5.

Additional Titles: Junior High/ Middle School Level

Alicia, My Story by Alicia Appleman-Jurman. (S)

Assignment: Rescue, An Autobiography by Varian Fry. (S)

The Big Lie: A True Story by Isabella Leitner with Irving A. Leitner. (E)

Children of the Resistance by Lore Cowan. (S)

Elie Wiesel: Messenger from the Holocaust by Carol Greene. (AL)

Father of the Orphans: The Story of Janusz Korczak by Mark Bernheim. (S)

In Kindling Flame: The Story of Hannah Senesh, 1921–1944 by Linda Atkinson. (S)

Raoul Wallenberg by Michael Nicholson and David Winner. (E)

Rescuers: Portraits of Moral Courage in the Holocaust by Gay
Block and Malka Drucker. (S)

So Young to Die: The Story of Hannah Senesh by Candice F. Ransom. (E)

Struggle by Sara Zyskind. (S)

Secondary School Level

Appleman-Jurman, Alicia. *Alicia, My Story.* Bantam Books, 1988. 356 pages.

Our life in the ghetto, the constant hunger, the gradual loss of family members, the horror of being hunted
by the Gestapo and killed, left very little hope of survival
in the hearts of Jewish children. I wasn't different from
the others. What kept me going was my love for my
mother and brother and the wish to see our murderers
punished for their crimes. There was a balance between
love and hate in my heart. Meeting Bella and her family
tipped the scale a little in the favor of love. (p. 61)

At a Glance ▪ Alicia Jurman tells the remarkable and heroic autobiography of her life from 1938 to 1947 as she survives the horrors
of the Holocaust in Poland. This book is appropriate for secondary
school students and some junior high/middle school readers.

Summary ▪ Alicia Jurman and her family lived a happy and successful life in eastern Poland. When Germany defeated Poland in
1939, she was nine years of age. During the next eight years, she
experienced the death of her father and then, one by one, her four
brothers, as the policy to terminate all Jews was brutally and systematically carried out by the Nazis. For a time, she and her mother
lived on the run, avoiding capture and foraging food where they
could. Alicia barely escaped death several times, and by age thirteen
she was helping others to survive. Tragically, near the end of World
War II, her mother was murdered by an SS officer as she saved
Alicia's life. After the war, Alicia was honored by the Russian Army
for helping the partisans. She established an orphanage at age 15
and then helped to smuggle Jews out of Poland. Determined to go

to Eretz, Israel, she was on a ship captured by the British and spent eight months in a camp on Cyprus before being allowed to enter the country.

Through the story of "Alicia" I wish to reach out, not only to survivors like myself, but to all people. I hope that it will help strengthen today's youth by imparting a better understanding of the true history of my whole lost generation. I believe that the book will teach young people what enormous reserves of strength they possess within themselves.

I pray that all its readers, Jews and non-Jews alike, may unite in the resolve that evil forces will never again be permitted to set one people against another. (p. 356)

Teaching Considerations ▪ Often students assume that the Holocaust ended with liberation of the camps and the defeat of Hitler in 1945. Help students to discover the period following the end of World War II. Some might want to explore the dislocation camps, others the immigration of survivors to other countries, or the establishment of the State of Israel. Landau's book, *We Survived the Holocaust*, is an appropriate follow-up to this book and is described in this chapter. Chapter 6 also has information on other titles relating to the postwar period.

Atkinson, Linda. *In Kindling Flame: The Story of Hannah Senesh, 1921–1944.* Lothrop, Lee & Shepard, 1985. 214 pages.

"I would like to be a great soul," Hannah wrote. "If God will permit!" (p. 15)

At a Glance ▪ This is a biography of Hannah Senesh, a young Hungarian Jew who became a legend when she was put to death for her work with the Resistance during World War II. The text also contains photographs and portions of Hannah's writings. The book received the National Jewish Book Award. It is appropriate for secondary school students and some junior high/middle school readers.

Summary ▪ Hannah Senesh was the privileged daughter of a prominent Hungarian family. She began to express herself through poetry and other forms of writing at the age of six after the death of her father, a well-known columnist and playwright. An excellent student, she became disillusioned and unsettled with the increasingly unjust treatment of Jews. Becoming a Zionist, she immigrated to Palestine after graduation. There she worked on several kibbutzim and gained a reputation for her hard work, ingenious ideas, and strong opinions. Tormented by what was happening to the Jews in Europe, she trained with the British in Egypt and parachuted into Nazi-occupied Yugoslavia to join the Resistance. Crossing into Hungary, she was captured, tortured, and later murdered. She is honored today as a martyr and for her courage and convictions.

> "There are stars whose radiance is visible on earth though they have long been extinct," Hannah wrote once. "There are people whose brilliance continues to light the world though they are no longer among the living. These lights are particularly bright when the night is dark. They light the way for humankind." (p. 206)

Teaching Considerations ▪ Hannah loved to write. It provided her with a way to understand her world through her poetry. Have your students select one of her poems that they particularly like and then have them write a poem of their own. Also, see the entries in this chapter on the other books about Hannah. Siegal's book, *Upon the Head of a Goat: A Childhood in Hungary, 1939–44,* could also serve as a companion to this book. For insight into the experiences of other young people in Hungary, have your students read *Young People Speak: Surviving the Holocaust in Hungary* by Handler and Meschel, described in this chapter.

Bernheim, Mark. *Father of the Orphans: The Story of Janusz Korczak.* Lodestar Books, 1989. 160 pages.

> Even in the darkest days of war, people can illuminate life through heroism and love. This is the story of one such person, a children's doctor and author . . . (p. 1)

At a Glance ▪ Janusz Korczak was a Polish doctor and author who devoted his life to the cause of serving children. He is well-known for the humane orphanages he established and his refusal to abandon his Warsaw orphans when the Nazis sent them to Treblinka where he, too, was murdered. This book is appropriate for secondary school students and some junior high/middle school students.

Summary ▪ Henryk Goldszmit was born in 1878 to a privileged Jewish family that was well-assimilated into Polish life and culture The family's fortunes changed dramatically when his father became mentally ill, and then went bankrupt when Henryk was eleven. He adopted Janusz Korczak as his non-Jewish pen name when he entered a prize-winning play in a competition at age twenty. Becoming a doctor, Korczak dedicated himself to helping homeless and destitute children. He was ahead of his time with his educational theories which proclaimed "the right of the child to respect." He was well-known and highly regarded as a physician, teacher, scientist, writer of children's stories and plays, pediatrician whose radio shows on raising children were popular, and founder of progressive and humane Christian and Jewish orphanages. When his Jewish orphanage was moved into the Warsaw Ghetto in 1940, he moved with it and eventually perished with the children in Treblinka.

> The story is that, at the last moment, the German commander recognized Korczak as the famous author whose books he had loved as a child, and offered the doctor a delay in deportation or even safety for himself if he would let the children go on alone. (p. 146)

Teaching Considerations ▪ Janusz Korczak was like many European Jews from wealthy families who were assimilated into their culture prior to World War II. Help your students to compare his experiences with others such as Hannah Senesh (see entries in this chapter). Some students will be interested in reading the novel, *Shadow of the Wall,* by Christa Laird, which describes the experiences of a boy in Dr. Korczak's orphanage in the Warsaw Ghetto (see chapter 4). The film *Korczak* can also be shown to students (see chapter 7.) For those students who want to learn more about the Warsaw Ghetto, recommend Israel Gutman's book, *Resistance: The Warsaw Ghetto Uprising;* to learn more about Treblinka, recommend Jean-François Steiner's book, *Treblinka,* (see chapter 2). Adam Gillon has edited *Poems of the Ghetto: A Testament of Lost Men* about life in the Warsaw Ghetto, described in this chapter.

Block, Gay, and Malka Drucker. *Rescuers: Portraits of Moral Courage in the Holocaust.*
Holmes and Meier, 1992. 255 pages.

> If you opt against opening your home and heart to an
> innocent fugitive, you have no place in the community
> of the just. (Pieter Miedema, p. 68)

At a Glance ▪ The authors, Block and Drucker, traveled to eight
countries and have interviewed more than 100 people who were
involved in rescuing Jews during the war. The interviews are accompanied by recent color photographs of the rescuers. The book
is appropriate for secondary school students and some junior high/
middle school students.

Summary ▪ This book presents interviews with people who resisted the terror and helped both friends and strangers to escape
from certain death at the hands of the Nazis. Each of these people
faced torture and death themselves if the Gestapo discovered that
they were giving aid to Jews. A recurring theme in these interviews
is the belief of many of these people that their actions were not in
any way extraordinary; they were simply the acts of decent human
beings.

> In May 1988, we organized a reunion of the boys and
> the teachers, and we arranged for Mme. Taquet to be
> honored by Yad Vashem. Many people came from all
> over the world to be at the castle to remember and pay
> homage to Mme. Taquet. Now I come to visit her and
> bring her cakes. She took care of me and now I must
> take care of her. For most of us it's the past, but as long
> as she lives, we have to be thankful. (p. 109)

Teaching Considerations ▪ Ask your students to select the interview that made the greatest impression on them and discuss why
they think so. Give them the opportunity to respond to the rescuers
by deciding what other questions they would like to ask them.
Show *The Courage to Care,* a documentary about ordinary people
who dared to help Holocaust victims (see chapter 7). Meltzer's *Rescue: The Story of How Gentiles Saved Jews in the Holocaust* is a
good companion to this book (see entry in this chapter).

Cowan, Lore. *Children of the Resistance.*
Meredith Press, 1969. 179 pages.

Arrangements were made secretly to round up the eight thousand Jews living in Denmark, and to transport them to concentration camps. The date fixed was the first of October, because this coincided with the Jewish New Year, and the Jewish families would be at home celebrating the holiday. A lightening raid would collar a lot. (p. 29)

At a Glance ▪ This book tells the heroic stories of youth who were involved in various Resistance movements throughout Europe in the struggle against Nazism. Appropriate for secondary school students and some junior high/middle school readers, this book will appeal to both genders.

Summary ▪ Although Lore Cowen does not deal exclusively with the horrors of the Holocaust, she does present a perspective on the pervasive evil of the Nazi regime as it filtered throughout Europe. She presents stories of youths who were involved in trying to stop the spread of Nazism. The book demonstrates that these acts of courage occurred throughout Europe and that there were always young people willing to embark on secret missions.

As the old man turned away to continue his solitary journey into the future, he was heard to murmur, "Not every German is a Nazi." (p. 179)

Teaching Considerations ▪ Have your students research the resistance movements. Have them discuss the roles young people played not only during the Holocaust, but during other times when a people or country was experiencing oppression. *Flames in the Ashes, Triumph of the Will,* or *Weapons of the Spirit* are films that could be shown to illustrate various types of resistance (see chapter 7).

Fry, Varian. *Assignment: Rescue, An Autobiography.*
Scholastic/United States Holocaust Memorial Museum, 1945, 1968. 183 pages.

"Sure, we know all about Fry," the German officer had said. "We know he's trying to get our political enemies out of France. We aren't worrying. We're confident he won't succeed."

This challenge was too difficult to ignore. I determined to prove them wrong. (p. 92)

At a Glance ▪ American Varian Fry tells of his thirteen months in Nazi-occupied France helping refugees to escape during 1940–41. Appropriate for secondary school students and some junior high/middle school readers, this exciting book will keep the interest of even reluctant readers.

Summary ▪ In 1940 a group of private citizens in New York formed the Emergency Rescue Committee to try to help musicians, artists, scientists, professors, writers, and political figures to escape from German-controlled France. Varian Fry was an unlikely person to send as a secret agent; he had no underground or secret agent experience and spoke only a little French with a decidedly American accent. Yet he was willing to risk his own life to help the enemies of the Third Reich to obtain false passports and other necessary papers, find escape routes and transportation, and secure money to escape imprisonment and death. In his 1992 introduction to this book, Dr. Albert O. Hirschman pays tribute to Varian Fry, who saved the lives of two to three thousand people in France during the Nazi occupation, calling him "a hero for our time."

> "Tell me frankly," I said. "Why are you so much opposed to me?"
>
> "Parce que vous avec trop protége juifs et des anti-Nazis," he said. "Because you have helped and protected Jews and anti-Nazis." (p. 173)

Teaching Considerations ▪ Have your students find out more about the Emergency Rescue Committee, its history, and its effectiveness. Have them find information about other rescue efforts. Ask them to consider why so few rescue efforts were undertaken. Students can also learn about the efforts of others who attempted to rescue the Jews, such as Raoul Wallenberg in Linnea book's *Raoul Wallenberg: The Man Who Stopped Death*, and those in Block and Drucker's *Rescuers: Portraits of Moral Courage in the Holocaust*, in this chapter. See also other entries in this chapter to help students learn more about some of the artists and poets who suffered during the Holocaust.

Wiesel, Elie. *Night.*
Hill & Wang, 1960, Bantam Books, 1982. Originally published in French. 109 pages.

> Within a few seconds, we had ceased to be men. If the situation had not been tragic, we should have roared with laughter. . . . I glanced at my father. How he had changed! His eyes had grown dim. I would have liked to speak to him, but I did not know what to say. (p. 34)

At a Glance ▪ Young Elie Wiesel was a scholarly and religious youth whose faith and beliefs were shattered by the brutality of the Holocaust. Wiesel's accounting is a thought-provoking one that would be most appropriate for more mature secondary school students.

Summary ▪ As a serious student of his faith, young Elie was always seeking answers to his questions. And he was told: "You will find the true answers, Eliezer, only within yourself!" (p. 3). But soon those questions changed as his world was invaded by the Nazis and he and his family were sent first into the ghetto and then transported to Auschwitz. In his vivid account of the conditions, the threats, and the fears with which they were forced to live in the camps, Wiesel transfixes the reader with his enduring sense of humanity that is manifested in his relationship with his father. At Auschwitz, Elie and his father were separated from his mother and sister and never saw either of them again. Juxtaposed against the story of the brutality of the Nazis is Elie's story of his relationship with his father and his absolute determination to stay with him until the end. The book is rich in its imagery, making the inhumanity of the Holocaust more real.

> I wanted to see myself in the mirror hanging on the opposite wall. I had not seen myself since the ghetto.
> From the depths of the mirror, a corpse gazed back at me. The look in his eyes, as they stared into mine, has never left me. (p. 109)

Teaching Considerations ▪ *Night* is one of the most highly regarded books about the Holocaust. Help students to look at its literary merit by discussing how the writing style contributes to the emotional impact of the work. Other authors they may want to read are Primo Levi and Victor Frankl (see entries in this chapter) and Otto Friedrich (see chapter 2). Greene's *Elie Wiesel: Messenger from the Holocaust,* also in this chapter, can be used as a general introduction to Wiesel and *Night.*

Zyskind, Sara. *Struggle.*
Lerner Publications, 1989. 284 pages.

"Luzer, I know that we're in the ghetto because we are Jews. But what have we done to the Germans that they should punish us? How are we different from those Polish girls who are free?"

I looked at my younger sister, now eight years old, at her big blue eyes, and I could find no answer. For I asked myself the very same question: What evil have we done to the Germans and the Poles who persecute us? How have we sinned towards them? We have always lived quietly and modestly. We worked hard to earn an honest living. Just what is so bad about having been born Jews? We are not murderers or thieves. Why then must we bear a badge of shame and be imprisoned behind barbed wire? But no one could answer. (p. 46)

At a Glance ▪ Sara Plager Zyskind provides a dramatic first-person account of her husband's struggles to stay alive as a teenager in Poland during the Holocaust. A riveting and powerful book that is appropriate for secondary school students and some junior high/ middle school students, it will have a special appeal to young male readers.

Summary ▪ Luzer, his younger sister, Talka, his parents and grandparents, and other relatives lived in a small town in Poland between Lodz and Warsaw. During the German invasion of Poland, their town was bombed and their home destroyed. Thus began their struggle to survive as they moved from place to place, and with each move survival became more tenuous. Throughout it all, their first priority was to stay together. They were forced to live first in a ghetto in their town, and then, when it is made *Judenrein* (Jew-free), the Lodz Ghetto where they were forced to provide labor for the Germans in exchange for meager rations of food. Eventually they were sent to Auschwitz where Luzer's parents and sister were put to death. Only his promise to his father to survive kept him alive as he was sent from camp to camp and on forced marches until liberation by Allied soldiers at the end of the war.

I asked myself what the concepts "enlightened man" and "enlightened and progressive world" meant if one wild man like Hitler could achieve leadership and spread a theory about racial superiority. . . . The enlightened world could not be silent in the face of the horrifying injustices performed against the Jews. (p. 137)

Teaching Considerations ▪ Luzer in Sara Zyskind's *Struggle* says, "The enlightened world could not be silent in the face of the horrifying injustices performed against the Jews"—and yet it was. Help your students to discuss why this happened. They may need to do additional research to understand this difficult issue. For students who want to know more about the Lodz Ghetto, recommend *With a Camera in the Ghetto* by Mendel Grossman (see chapter 2). *Lodz Ghetto*, a documentary, can also be shown to students (see chapter 7). *Lodz Ghetto: Inside a Community Under Siege*, compiled and edited by Alan Adelson and Robert Lapides, is a source book for the film. It is annotated in this chapter.

Additional Titles: Secondary School Level

Clara's Story by Clara Isaacman as told to Joan Adess Grossman. (JM)

Elie Wiesel: Messenger from the Holocaust by Carol Greene. (AL)

Hiding to Survive: Stories of Jewish Children Rescued from the Holocaust by Maxine B. Rosenberg. (JM)

I Am a Star: Child of the Holocaust by Inge Auerbacher. (JM)

Rescue: The Story of How Gentiles Saved Jews in the Holocaust by Milton Meltzer. (JM)

The Survivor in Us All: Four Young Sisters in the Holocaust by Erna F. Rubinstein. (JM)

Upon the Head of a Goat: A Childhood in Hungary, 1939–44 by Aranka Siegal. (JM)

Further Reading for All Levels

Adelson, Alan, and Robert Lapides, comps. and eds. *Lodz Ghetto: Inside a Community Under Siege*. Viking, 1989. 526 pages. (S)

The source book for the film of the same title (see chapter 7), this is a collection of personal writings and photographs that document life in the Lodz Ghetto. In 1940, the 200,000 Jews of Lodz were forced into the ghetto; in 1941, they were joined by another 20,000 Jews from other European nations. At the end of the war, almost no one remained. The editors of this book, under the auspices of the Jewish Heritage Project, collected the writings and photographs of the ghetto inhabitants from all over the world—diaries, poetry, notebooks, and sketches that chronicle the destruction of this community.

Adler, David A. *Child of the Warsaw Ghetto*. Illustrated by Karen Ritz. Holiday House, 1995. 30 pages. (E, JM, P)

Using the actual experiences of Erwin (Froim) Baum, Adler and Ritz have created another powerful picture book about the Holocaust. Told through the eyes of a young Jewish boy, this account of the Warsaw Ghetto is more appropriate for older readers than for young children who have little or no background knowledge of the Holocaust. The gray tint of the paper and illustrations contribute greatly to creating an appropriate mood for understanding the horrifying personal consequences of this period in history.

Baldwin, Margaret. *The Boy Who Saved the Children*. Julian Messner, 1981. 63 pages. (E, JM)

The Jews confined to the Lodz Ghetto lived in fear of an "Action," when the German soldiers would come through and select people to be sent to the death camps who were too young, too old, or too ill. Only those workers who were strong enough to aid the war effort survived. Young Ben Edelbaum worked in a factory making fur coats for the Nazis when he heard the rumor that all children were to be rounded up and sent away. This is the exciting account of how Ben struggled to find a way to save his workers and himself.

Bernbaum, Israel. *My Brother's Keeper: The Holocaust Through the Eyes of an Artist*. G. P. Putnam's Sons, 1985. 64 pages. (S)

Israel Bernbaum escaped from his native Warsaw shortly before the Nazis imprisoned Jews in the Warsaw Ghetto. His paintings pay tribute to those who perished there and everywhere throughout the reign of Hitler. In this book, his series of five Warsaw Ghetto paintings are used to create powerful and painful images of the times and the treatment of Jews. Bernbaum frequently juxtaposes his ghetto images with images of life outside the walls, dramatizing the horrors that Jews lived under. He describes the different images in each of his paintings and relates their symbolic significance. Bernbaum also includes some of the actual photographs of the ghetto that inspired parts of his paintings.

Drucker, Malka, and Michael Halperin. *Jacob's Rescue*. Dell Publishing, 1993. 117 pages. (E)

Jacob Gutgeld's life of comfort was disrupted when the Nazis overran Poland. He and his family were sent to the Warsaw Ghetto when he was nine. His family had been wealthy before the Nazis took over, but they retained some loyal friends, including one who found a Christian family who agreed to take Jacob and hide him in their home. His new "family" was at risk but they protected Jacob and eventually his younger brothers.

Drucker, Olga Levy. *Kindertransport*. Henry Holt, 1992. 146 pages. (E, JM)

After *Kristallnacht*, many German Jewish parents sent their children to England for safekeeping. Levy describes her experiences of arriving in England at age eleven, not knowing anyone or the language, and living there without her parents for six years.

Fluek, Toby Knobel. *Memories of My Life in a Polish Village, 1930–1949*. Alfred A. Knopf, 1990. 110 pages. (E, JM)

Fluek uses drawings and paintings of the scenes from her early life to accompany short descriptions of events, places, and people from her past. While many of the Holocaust books end with or shortly after liberation, this book illustrates that the hardships continued through relocation and immigration to other countries.

Frank, Anne. *Anne Frank's Tales from the Secret Annex*. Washington Square Press, 1952, 1959, 1983. 156 pages. (JM)

The collection of stories, fables, essays, and an unfinished novel that compose this work captures the same zeal and joy, and conveys the same insights, that readers of her *Diary* have come to know. Perhaps these two collections of Anne Frank's writings provide readers with the most vivid human face of the times.

Frank, Anne. *The Diary of a Young Girl.* Translated from the Dutch by B.M. Mooyaart. Doubleday, 1952, 1967; Bantam Books, 1986. 283 pages. (JM)

Parts of this work are included in various forms in many middle school anthologies. For some students, Anne Frank is their major frame of reference for the Holocaust. The *Diary* remains a remarkable account of a sensitive young woman.

Frankl, Victor. *Man's Search for Meaning: An Introduction to Logotherapy.* Originally published as *From Death-Camp to Existentialism.* Beacon Press, 1959, 1962. (S)

Frankl's book is a tribute to the human spirit and its ability to overcome the most heinous circumstances. It is one man's quest to establish a sense of meaning for and in life while imprisoned in Auschwitz. Under conditions designed to humiliate, dehumanize, and ultimately destroy the individual, Frankl not only survived, but he also found a personal sense of meaning that he developed into a school of psychotherapy called "logotherapy" or "existential analysis." This book is appropriate for teachers and advanced secondary school students.

Friedman, Ina R. *The Other Victims: First-Person Stories of Non-Jews Persecuted by the Nazis.* Houghton Mifflin, 1990. 214 pages. (JM, S)

Many groups besides the Jews were persecuted and marked for extermination by the Nazis. Ina Friedman traveled extensively to interview Gypsies, Slavs, blacks, homosexuals, handicapped people, and others who had been labeled "undesirables." Their personal stories are told in this book.

Gies, Miep, and Alison Leslie Gold. *Anne Frank Remembered.* Simon and Schuster, 1987. 252 pages. (S, JM)

This book presents the other side of the most famous case of the hiding of Jews during the Holocaust. Most often stories of this kind are from the perspective of those who are hiding, but this is told by Miep Gies, who hid the Frank family. She was an employee of Otto

Frank's, but more important, she served as their lifeline during the years the family spent in the attic. She was their regular contact with the world; it was she who brought them food and news of what was happening. When the war was over she and her husband provided a home for Otto Frank. She returned Anne's diary, which has become one of the most famous works about the Holocaust, to her father.

Gillon, Adam, ed. *Poems of the Ghetto: A Testament of Lost Men.* Twayne, 1969. 96 pages. (S, JM)

From this slim book of poems about the Warsaw Ghetto rise the voices of courage and of pain. The poems represent the work of acknowledged Polish poets and some whose names were lost forever in the carnage. The book is filled with powerful poems in which the imagery is sometimes shocking and painful.

Greenfeld, Howard. *The Hidden Children.* Ticknor and Fields, 1993. 118 pages. (JM, E)

Greenfeld tells of the Holocaust, focusing on the survival of children who were hidden from the Nazis. He puts a human face on the times by including personal accounts of the experiences of fifteen men and women who spent part of their childhood denying their Jewish heritage as they hid. Greenfeld effectively provides an historical background for the remembrances.

Handler, Andrew, and Susan V. Meschel, comps. and eds. *Young People Speak: Surviving the Holocaust in Hungary.* Franklin Watts, 1993. 160 pages. (S, JM)

Although Hungary was able to remain relatively free of German dominance until it was invaded and conquered in 1944, over 75 percent of its Jewish population, approximately 600,000 people, perished once the Nazis were in control. This books presents the memories of eleven individuals who survived the Holocaust in Hungary. All of them were children who were able to remain out of the camps and survived by living in the ghettos, hiding and avoiding capture, while suffering terrible hardships and the loss of loved ones.

Jens, Inge, comp. *At the Heart of the White Rose: Letters and Diaries of Hans and Sophie Scholl.* Harper & Row, 1987. 331 pages. (S)

Gentile brother and sister Hans and Sophie Scholl take action against Hitler when they and a small group of friends form the White Rose, a resistance group that revealed the truth about the actions of the Third Reich. They were arrested in 1943 and executed, but their letters and diaries remain to demonstrate their commitment to humanity.

Koehn, Ilse. *MISCHLING, Second Degree: My Childhood in Nazi Germany.* Greenwillow Books, 1977; Puffin Books, 1990. 240 pages. (S, JM)

In Nazi Germany, Hitler's hatred of Jews was so extreme that he established a system for identifying anyone of Jewish heritage whether they were practicing their religion or not. The Nuremberg Laws of 1935 created categories of Jews. Anyone with even one Jewish grandparent was labeled as a *Mischling, Second Degree.* This was the case of Ilse who was only six at the time. Since her family did not practice any religion and politically were anti-Nazi, the Koehns sought to protect their daughter. She lived with her maternal grandparents in the country outside of Berlin and was involved in all of the regular activities that a young person in Nazi Germany would experience. While she knew that her family did not believe in the Nazi philosophy, she never knew that she was at risk because of her heritage. Her father even kept the cause of her paternal grandmother's murder by the Nazis from her until after the war was over and the family was reunited. This book presents a vivid picture of the attempt of the Nazis to take control of the minds of young people. Some of the language in the book might be offensive to young readers. The details of the historical setting and the times make the book more appropriate for secondary school students and some junior high/middle school readers.

Korwin, Yala. *To Tell the Story: Poems of the Holocaust.* Holocaust Library, 1987. 112 pages. (S, JM)

These poems reflect Yala Korwin's experiences and memories of the Holocaust. Born in Poland, her father was a scholar, writer, and teacher; Yala was an art student. When the Nazis took over, her family attempted to live outside of the ghetto. She and her younger sister survived by passing as "Aryans" and working in a labor camp. The rest of her family perished.

Kulka, Erich. *Escape from Auschwitz*. Bergin & Garvey, 1986. 151 pages. (S)

Escapes from Auschwitz were attempted many times, but almost always resulted in death. Erich Kulka, a survivor of Auschwitz, fictionalizes the true story of Siegfried Lederer and his successful escape.

Landau, Elaine. *We Survived the Holocaust*. Franklin Watts, 1991. 144 pages. (S, JM)

This book is a collection of the memoirs of sixteen Jewish Holocaust survivors from Germany, Poland, Austria, Holland, Hungary, Czechoslovakia, and Transylvania. It includes photos of each individual from then and now. These accounts tell of their experiences as young people desperately seeking to escape the Nazis' "Final Solution."

Levi, Primo. *Survival in Auschwitz: The Nazi Assault on Humanity*. Orion Press, 1960; Collier Books, 1986. (S)

This book, a classic of twentieth-century literature, is a powerful and sensitively written account of the experiences of one man who examines his circumstances and reflects upon them. Levi was a young research chemist when he was transported to Auschwitz. His rational, scientific view and understanding helped him to survive. This book is one that teachers should read to gain an understanding of the horror of the imprisonment. The allusions in and metaphorical nature of this book make it difficult reading, so it is appropriate only for advanced secondary school students. Some of Levi's other works are *The Reawakening* and *Moments of Reprieve, A Memoir of Auschwitz*

Linnea, Sharon. *Raoul Wallenberg: The Man Who Stopped Death*. Jewish Publication Society, 1993. 151 pages. (JM, S)

Raoul Wallenberg went to Hungary as a member of the Swedish Legation but his real mission was on behalf of the War Refugee Board of the United States. With the help of the Red Cross, he was responsible for saving 100,000 Hungarian Jews. His brave defiance of the Nazis and Adolf Eichmann made him a hero to all freedom-loving people.

Neimark, Anne E. *One Man's Valor: Leo Baeck and the Holocaust*. E.P. Dutton, 1986. 113 pages. (JM, E)

Leo Baeck, a highly respected Jewish leader, scholar, and rabbi, helped many Jews to escape from Germany during the Holocaust. Even though he had opportunities to flee, he stayed to help others. Arrested five times, he was sent eventually to the Theresienstadt concentration camp where he continued to help others through his example and courage. The postwar welfare of European Jews became his great concern after liberation. Baeck was the first prominent German Jew to make a return visit to Germany. He is considered to be one of the foremost Jewish thinkers and theologians of the twentieth century.

Nir, Yehuda. *The Lost Childhood: A Memoir.* Harcourt Brace
    Jovanovich, 1989. 256 pages. (S)

Yehuda Nir tells the story of his life from 1939, when he was a nine-year-old Polish Jewish boy in an affluent home, until 1945, when he and his mother and sister were liberated. During those six years, they survived dangers and hardships, including the murder of his father. Living by their wits, they obtained false identity papers and passed themselves off as Polish Catholics. In Warsaw, they were relatively safe for awhile working for Germans until Yehuda joined the Polish volunteer resistance army. When the rebellion was put down, they were sent to a German labor camp. They survived by their wits as they went to work again for their former employers, this time in Germany itself.

Pettit, Jayne. *A Place to Hide: True Stories of Holocaust Rescues.*
    Scholastic, 1993. 114 pages. (JM, E)

The epilogue to this book quotes author Philip P. Hallie: "Rescue is not always accompanied by blazing guns and blaring bugles. Sometimes the quiet kind can be just as effective—and just as dangerous" (p. 105). This book tells the stories of Euopeans who risked their lives to help Jews during the Holocaust. Some of the stories are of well-known people such as Oskar and Emilie Schindler and Miep Gies, who hid Anne Frank's family, while others are unknown people such as Jonka Kowalyk who hid fourteen Ukrainian Jews for two years in the attic of her family's house in a small farm village near a Nazi camp. The stories are exciting and inspiring and lend themselves well to being read aloud.

Ramati, Alexander. *And the Violins Stopped Playing: A Story of
    the Gypsy Holocaust.* Franklin Watts, 1986. 237 pages. (S)

Based on the personal narratives of a Gypsy who contacted him after the war, Ramati's account of the Gypsy persecution by the Germans reads like a novel. The Gypsies thought that they were safe from the Nazis because they were also Aryans, but this assumption proved to be dangerously untrue. This book helps the reader to understand the customs and lifestyle of the Gypsies as well as the extent of the Nazi desire to produce a "pure race" of people.

Rittner, Carol, R.S.M., and Sondra Myers, eds. *The Courage to Care: Rescuers of Jews During the Holocaust.* New York University Press, 1986. 157 pages. (JM, S, E)

This book contains photos, short personal narratives and essays about efforts to rescue Jews during the Holocaust. The stories range from individual efforts to those of an entire village. Five short essays by writers such as Elie Wiesel provide readers with opportunities to reflect upon these experiences and related questions. This book has appeal for a wide range of readers. It could be effectively read aloud to students. A film of the same title is also available (see chapter 7).

Rothchild, Sylvia, ed. *Voices from the Holocaust.* Meridian Books, 1982. 456 pages. (S)

Rothchild has compiled the accounts of Jews living in the United States as they reflect on their lives before, during, and after the Holocaust. Materials from the William E. Wiener Oral History Library of the American Jewish Committee are used in this text.

Roth-Hano, Renée. *Touch Wood: A Girlhood in Occupied France.* Four Winds Press; Puffin Books, 1988. 297 pages. (JM, S)

Renée Roth-Hano uses a diary format to tell the true story of her life after the German invasion and occupation of France. As life becomes increasing dangerous for Jews, her parents arrange for her and her sisters to live in a Catholic residence for women in Normandy. This book is an ALA Notable Book.

Schur, Maxine. *Hannah Szenes—A Song of Light.* Jewish Publication Society, 1986. 106 pages. (JM, S)

This is the biography of Hannah Senesh, a young Hungarian Jew and poet, who parachutes into Yugoslavia to work with the Resistance. Captured after returning to Hungary to try to help save Jews, she became a legend when she was put to death by the Nazis.

Spiegelman, Art. *Maus, A Survivor's Tale*. Pantheon Books. 1973. 159 pages. (S)

Spiegelman chronicles in a cartoon strip format the experiences that his parents had during the Holocaust. He traces his parents' lives from their courtship until the time they were taken to Auschwitz. The Jews are portrayed as mice while the Nazis are cats setting huge and horrible traps like Auschwitz/ Birkenau. The story of the parents' trials and hardships are juxtaposed with the relationship between father and son and Spiegelman's efforts to understand and come to terms with his father.

Spiegelman, Art. *Maus II , A Survivor's Tale and Here My Troubles Began*. Pantheon Books. 1986. 135 pages. (S)

In this sequel to *Maus, A Survivor's Tale,* Spiegelman continues the tale of horror that his parents endured during the Holocaust. As Spiegelman recounts their experiences, he also relates the experiences he had with his father during his father's last illness. This story is truly one of survival—survival in the camps and survival of a survivor's son who grew up with the specter of the camps and of the brother who perished while he was in hiding during the war.

Stein, R. Conrad. *World at War: Warsaw Ghetto*. Children's Press, 1985. 47 pages. (E, JM)

This brief account focuses on the incarceration of Jews in the ghetto of Warsaw, the largest of the Jewish ghettoes during Hitler's reign. Warsaw, prior to the German invasion, had the largest Jewish population of any European city. From September 1939 when the Germans took control of Poland until 1943, thousands of Jews were killed in Warsaw or after having been sent from Warsaw to the death camp at Treblinka. The spring of 1943 was particularly bloody because a group of young people smuggled in arms and explosives and decided to fight the German guards of the ghetto. This book relates the story of the Warsaw Ghetto uprising in which a number of the remaining members of the Jewish community took arms and fought to the death against insurmountable odds. There are a number of photographs that add to the book's poignancy.

ten Boom, Corrie, with John and Elizabeth Sherrill. *The Hiding Place*. Chosen Books, 1971; Bantam Books, 1974. 219 pages. (S, JM)

Corrie ten Boom, a devout middle-aged Christian, lived a quiet life with her sister and elderly father above their watch shop in Haarlem, Holland. Their lives changed dramatically when Corrie became involved in underground activities and they hid Jews in their home from the Nazis. Eventually, they were arrested and sent to a German concentration camp. Corrie was the only one to survive, but her faith became an inspiration to others.

Toll, Nelly S. *Behind the Secret Window: A Memoir of a Hidden Childhood During World War Two*. Dial Books, 1993. 161 pages. (JM, E)

When Nelly Toll was eight, she and her mother were hidden from the Nazis by a Christian couple for thirteen months in Poland. During that time, Nelly kept a journal of her experiences and painted sixty-four watercolors. This book contains reproductions of twenty-nine of her paintings. It received the 1994 International Reading Association Children's Book Award.

Volavkova, Hana, ed. . . . *I Never Saw Another Butterfly* . . . Expanded second edition by the United States Holocaust Memorial Museum. Schocken Books, 1993. 106 pages. Originally published for the State Jewish Museum in Prague, 1959. (S, JM)

This is a poignant collection of the poetry, diary entries, and artwork created by the young people who were imprisoned in the Terezin concentration camp from 1942 to 1944. These young people were given classes and art lessons as therapy to help them to cope with the horrible realities of their lives. The artwork should be used with the writings to present a more complete experience. This work has also been adapted as drama (see chapter 5).

Weinstein, Frida Scheps. *A Hidden Childhood, A Jewish Girl's Sanctuary in a French Convent, 1942–1945*. Translated by Barbara Loeb Kennedy. Hill and Wang, 1983, 1985. 152 pages. (JM, S)

Frida Scheps writes from her personal experiences as a young Jewish child in France during the Geman occupation. Sent to a Catholic convent school at the Chateau de Beaujeu for her own safety, she is fascinated by the Church and its teachings, but troubled by her memories of life with her mother in Paris. While the reading level is appropriate for junior high/middle school students, secondary school students may find the religious issues interesting.

Zar, Rose. *In the Mouth of the Wolf*. Jewish Publication Society of America, 1983. 225 pages. (S, JM)

The author tells how she saved herself during the Holocaust by hiding "in the mouth of the wolf." Ruska Guterman (Rose Zar) escaped from a Polish ghetto and lived by her wits, hiding her Jewishness, and performing a number of functions, even working as a housekeeper for an SS officer.

Literature Involvement:
Suggestions and Issues for Responding and Thinking

Reading biographies and personal memoirs of the Holocaust is often a powerful experience for young people. They need opportunities to reflect upon what they are learning and to express their feelings. They also need opportunities to clarify misconceptions and to seek additional information. The following suggestions can be selected according to their appropriateness for the various age groups and then used to provide these opportunities:

- After having read some of the biographies or personal narratives recommended in this chapter, go back to your original definitions and discussions of what a hero is and the characteristics of a hero. How have your views been reinforced or changed by reading these books? What have you learned about the different ways people responded to the terrorism of the Nazis toward the Jewish people and others during World War II?

- Develop a profile of one of the individuals that you read about from the books recommended in this chapter.

- Design a collage that represents the life of one of the individuals that you read about from the books recommended in this chapter.

- Analyze several of the individuals from the books you have read. What personal characteristics do they have in common? How do they differ?

- Select an incident from the experiences of one of the individuals you have read about from the books recommended in this chapter. Dramatize that incident either by yourself or with other members of the class.

- Select a quote from one of the individuals in the books you read. What does it reveal about that individual? What impact does it have on you? (In a classroom setting, students can write their quotes on the chalkboard or on paper strips to display on the walls. These quotes then can be used to prompt group discussion and as a springboard for writing.)

- Prepare a list of questions to serve as a guide and then make an appointment to interview a survivor of the Holocaust. Find out how that person spent the war years. Remember that the survivors were not just those who were in the camps, but also those who were in hiding and in the resistance.

- Discuss the various reasons why many Jews did not flee when Hitler and the Nazis began restricting their rights or when conditions continued to deteriorate.

- There was a long and painful tradition in early European history to isolate Jews into ghettoes. Explore this aspect of history and relate it to the ghettoes of the Third Reich. Do ghettoes exist today?

- Find several adults who lived during World II who are willing to let you interview them about what they remember about that time. Ask if they have photographs they would be willing to let you see. If appropriate, write a description of a specific incident from one of their lives.

- As you read biographies, autobiographies, and personal narratives from the Holocaust, you may have asked yourself, "What would I have done? How would I have acted?" Discuss your feelings and reactions with someone else.

- Why is it so important for survivors to tell others about their experiences?

- Express in a creative format something significant that you have learned about someone who lived during the Holocaust. Examples of types of creative expression include the visual arts, music, creative dramatics, dance, poetry, or other forms of writing.

4

We Learn from Stories

Historical Fiction

> Fiction cannot recite the numbing numbers, but it can be
> that witness, that memory. A storyteller can attempt to tell
> the human tale, can make a galaxy out of the chaos, can
> point to the fact that some people survived even as most
> people died. And can remind us that swallows still sing
> around the smokestacks.
>
> Jane Yolen, *The Devil's Arithmetic*

This chapter presents historical fiction based on the actual events
of the Holocaust and the experiences of real people who lived then.
Historical fiction is a powerful way to help readers experience unfa-
miliar times, events, and conditions. By definition, historical fiction
relies upon accuracy about the period in which it is set; demonstrates a sense of the chronology of the times; presents historical
figures consistent with their documented behavior; and recreates a
believable, vivid impression of the times. The period from 1933 to
1945 marked the apex of inhumanity in modern times. Historical
fiction uses the factual basis of this time and puts a human face on
it by giving young readers characters with whom they can identify.

Fiction has the potential to transport readers and to help them feel
as well as understand the travails and triumphs of the characters.

The connection between readers and characters is a vital one, so vital that readers often speak of books that have had lasting impact on them or that have even changed their lives. That connection reaffirms the importance of literature as a means of understanding our world. The horrors of the Holocaust are overwhelming even for those of us who did not directly experience it. The statistics are staggering, but hearing of the fate of six million faceless people does not have the personal impact that the story of one individual does. The literature that we examine in this section will have a special impact on youthful readers because in every case the main character or characters are themselves youths, thus heightening the potential for the readers to make connections with them. These works, with their basis in reality and historical fact, create a human and a humane perspective to the monumental tragedy of the Holocaust.

Historical fiction teaches lessons, the lessons of the past. Again we are reminded of the words of philosopher George Santayana, "Those who cannot remember the past are condemned to repeat it." Christopher Collier, author of historical fiction for young people, has talked about the nature of historical fiction in this light. He contends that it not only teaches, but it also reaffirms and transmits the values of a culture. One only has to look at the literature of the Holocaust to confirm his belief. The values of freedom, courage, perseverance, and faith are among the pervasive values that are consistent throughout the body of books for young people.

An important aspect of the works included in this section as well as in other sections is that they reflect the range of experiences that young people had during the Holocaust. Some spent months and years in hiding; others were involved in resistance activities; some were on the move fleeing from one country to another, always trying to elude the deadly arm of Nazism; and for still another group, existence was a daily battle to stay alive in the concentration camps of the Third Reich. Regardless of their experiences, they were all at war and it took great courage and tenacity to survive. Unfortunately, even great courage and tenacity were not enough for the millions who were sacrificed.

Prior to Reading: Think About . . .

Historical fiction can be a tremendous influence in helping young people learn about the Holocaust. The elements of well-written fiction help readers to experience vicariously events that happened a long time ago. It is important to help readers identify with these events and to think about their consequences for our lives today. The following questions can be used to prompt this discussion:

- What is historical fiction? How is it different from an informational book? How is it similiar?

- How is it different from a biography or personal narrative? How is it similar?

- Why do some authors choose to tell their stories through historical fiction rather than as informational books, biographies, or personal narratives?

- Do you prefer one type of book over another (informational, fiction, biography/personal narrative)? Why?

- Think of a situation in which you or some of your family members were treated unfairly. What actions did you take? What actions did you want to take, but didn't or couldn't? Explain how your actions and inactions made you feel, and why?

- Read the quotes listed below from the book you have chosen. What do you think they mean? What do you think they reveal about the story?

Focus: We Learn from Stories

Best Friend by Elisabeth Reuter. (P, E)

Bridge to Freedom by Isabel L. Marvin. (JM, E)

Daniel's Story by Carol Matas. (JM, E, S)

Devil's Arithmetic by Jane Yolen. (JM, S, E)

Hide and Seek by Ida Vos. (JM, E)

Journey to America by Sonia Levitin. (E, JM)

The Lily Cupboard by Levey Oppenheim. (P)

Lisa's War by Carol Matas. (S, JM)

The Man from the Other Side by Uri Orlev. (S, JM)

Number the Stars by Lois Lowry. (E, JM)

Rose Blanche by Roberto Innocenti. (AL)

Sheltering Rebecca by Mary Baylis-White. (E, JM)

Twenty and Ten by Claire Huchet Bishop. (E, JM)

Waiting for Anya by Michael Morpurgo. (E, JM)

All School Levels

Innocenti, Roberto. *Rose Blanche.*
Creative Education, 1985. 28 pages.

> Suddenly, electric barbed wire stopped me. Behind it
> there were some children standing still. I didn't know
> any of them. The youngest said they were hungry. Since
> I had a piece of bread, I carefully handed it to them
> through the pointed wires. (unnumbered)

At a Glance ▪ This award-winning picture book depicts War
World II through the eyes of a young German girl. It is powerful
and poignant, and appropriate for all ages.

Summary ▪ Rose Blanche is a young schoolgirl who lives in a small
German town. German soldiers arrive and the townspeople fly Nazi
flags. One day Rose Blanche sees a young boy captured and put in
a truck by the soldiers. She quietly follows the truck to a forbidden
area outside town where she discovers a concentration camp. She
gives the hungry children behind the barbed wire a piece of bread
and secretly returns as often as she can with more food. Then the
course of the war changes and the German soldiers and townspeople flee as Russian soldiers advance. Rose Blanche is caught in the
crossfire. The story ends on a note of hope with the arrival of
spring.

> Shadows were moving between the trees. It was hard to
> see them. Soldiers saw the enemy everywhere. There was
> a shot. (unnumbered)

Teaching Considerations ▪ This powerful book usually evokes
strong emotions. Read it aloud and then give the students an oppor-

tunity to express their feelings through writing or artistic expression. Have them select an illustration that made a significant impression on them and describe why they chose it. Sometimes older students use their experience with this book as a springboard to research some of the camps to discover what the local people said about them or if they knew what was happening in the camps.

Primary School Level

Oppenheim, Levey. Illustrated by Ronald Himler.
The Lily Cupboard.
HarperCollins, 1992. 28 pages.

"It will be much easier for Papa and me to take care of ourselves knowing that you are hidden away in the country." (unnumbered)

At a Glance ▪ Miriam, a young Jewish child, is sent to the country to hide with a non-Jewish family. This beautifully illustrated picture book is appropriate to read to primary school children.

Summary ▪ When the Nazis invade Holland, Miriam's parents decide she must be sent to the country to hide with a non-Jewish family. Miriam becomes friends with their son, Nello, and together they take care of a rabbit. In the time they spend together, they try to understand what war is. One day Nazi soldiers come to the farm and Miriam must hide in a secret hiding place the family has prepared for her, a cupboard with lilies painted on it. Seen through the eyes of a young girl, this book will help young children to identify with the suffering and heroism of this time in history.

But even in these dark times there were many heroes. (unnumbered)

Teaching Considerations ▪ This book can be read aloud several times to young children as they discover the various levels of meaning. Children may initially relate to Miriam's fears at being away from her parents. Help them to talk about what parents do today to help their children be safe and compare that with what parents had to do during the Holocaust. You can also lead them in a discussion of heroes. Since television and the movies often present a distorted view of heroism for young people, help them to see the heroic behavior in this book.

Reuter, Elisabeth. *Best Friend.*
Yellow Brick Road Press, 1993. Originally published in German.
25 pages.

It felt good to have someone to blame for everything
that went wrong. (unnumbered)

At a Glance ▪ Lisa and Judith are closest friends until the Nazis
change things. This book is appropriate to read aloud to primary
students. While elementary school students will be able to read it
independently, they will still need some help in understanding the
context of the times.

Summary ▪ Judith and Lisa, who lives across the street, have always done everything together. After the Nazis come into power
and the persecution of Jews begins, their teacher says that Jews are
bad. Judith does not understand why people are suddenly angry
with her. Lisa is puzzled by the new reactions to her friend. The
girls continue to try to do things together, but it becomes increasingly difficult. When Lisa's parents decide that she should have
other friends, the girls find a way to play together when they are
not around. But then things become even worse.

Something terrible had happened but Lisa could not understand what it was. (unnumbered)

Teaching Considerations ▪ Introduce this book by having students
talk about what it means to be best friends. Provide students with
a brief summary of the historical context of the times at a level that
they can understand. Although this book is sometimes criticized for
slight historical distortions, its strength lies in helping students to
begin to explore and understand the concept of scapegoating ("It
felt good to have someone to blame for everything that went
wrong."). Help students to apply this concept to familiar experiences.

Additional Titles: Primary School Level

Rose Blanche by Roberto Innocenti. (AL)

Elementary School Level

Baylis-White, Mary. *Sheltering Rebecca.*
Lodestar Books, 1991; Puffin Books, 1993. 99 pages.

"In Germany now, to be Jewish is to be bad people. They shout at us, they break our windows, Papi cannot teach at the university, we cannot buy things in some shops . . ." Rebecca's voice faded away. The scowl she had so often came back to her face. "I must not think about it. I cannot help Mami and Papi and Helmut. Mrs. Trevelyan tells me this. I do not know." (p. 25)

At a Glance ▪ When Clarissa goes to spend her holidays with her grandparents, she has a school assignment to learn about her ancestors. Her grandmother Sally tells her about growing up in England during World War II when her best friend was a Jewish refugee who came to her home town. This book is appropriate for elementary school children and some junior high school/middle school students.

Summary ▪ For Sally, growing up in England in the late 1930s, Hitler and the Nazis are a vague awareness. The reality of Germany comes to her and to her small town when Rebecca Muller arrives. Rebecca's parents have sent her away after her older brother is arrested by the Nazis on his way home from school. Smuggled out of Germany by Mrs. Trevelyan, the English town's mayor, Rebecca has to learn a new language and adjust to being away from home. Sally is asked to help her. With the outbreak of war, Rebecca fears that she has lost her whole family. With Sally's help and friendship, Rebecca begins to make a new life in England, but not without difficulties. The story reflects life in England throughout the war.

"This is a wicked play. Yes, wicked. Your wonderful Shakespeare was just another Jew-hater. Why do you all hate us?" Rebecca stood up, furious. (p. 90)

Teaching Considerations ▪ This book is composed of a number of short episodes that present insights about events during World War II. Have students select one episode and write a scene that they think might follow it. A good companion book is *Kindertransport* by Olga Levy Drucker in which the author describes her experiences of being sent as a child from Germany to England for safe-keeping (see chapter 3). Have students compare the similarities and differences between the two books.

Bishop, Claire Huchet. Illustrated by William Pène du Bois.
Twenty and Ten. **Viking Press, 1952; Puffin Books, 1978; Viking Penguin, 1991. 76 pages.**

> "Boys and girls," he said, "I have to speak to you just as if you were adults. You know that the Germans occupy France. You know also about the refugees and the DPs?" We nodded. "Now, do you know that there are people who not only are refugees and DPs but have ab-solutely no place to go, because if the Nazis find them they will kill them?" (pp. 19–20)

At a Glance ▪ During the Nazi occupation of France, twenty chil-dren and their teacher, Sister Gabriel, hide Jewish children. When the Nazis arrive, the class faces the challenge of keeping the pres-ence of the Jewish children a secret. This book is appropriate for elementary school students and some junior high/middle school readers.

Summary ▪ The title *Twenty and Ten* refers to the nineteen fifth-graders (and one younger brother) who are joined by ten refugee children whom they hide from the Nazis. The fifth-graders are all housed in a beautiful old home on a hillside in the country. A small group from the class, joined by one of the refugee children, dis-covers a large, dry cave that will hold fifteen people. This discovery proves to be fortunate because a short time later, their teacher goes into town, thinking that the Nazis have gone away. The Nazis ar-rest her and send two soldiers to the house on the hill to look for the refugee children. How long will the others be able to keep the secret while they hide in the cave?

> The other soldier took Henry by the shoulders and pushed him out of the room. Henry managed to throw a glance at us. He was very pale; his fists were clenched, his lips tight, and in his eyes we read, "Hold on!" The door closed behind them. (p.117)

Teaching Considerations ▪ This book can lead to a discussion of how survival in Nazi-occupied Europe often depended upon se-crecy. Help your students describe what they might have done and felt in the situations described in the book. Have them write a jour-nal entry (either from an actual experience or an imaginary one) discussing an experience in which they had to kept a secret. Excerpts from Rosenberg's *Hiding to Survive: Stories of Jewish Children Rescued from the Holocaust,* Toll's *Behind the Secret Window: A Memoir of a Hidden Childhood During World War Two,* and Greenfield's *The Hidden Children,* as well as one of the books about Anne Frank, are appropriate companions to this book (see chapter 3).

Levitin, Sonia. *Journey to America.* Atheneum, 1970. 150 pages. (E, JM)

"They say that nobody should take Hitler seriously, and it's silly for people to move away, because it will all blow over." (p. 9)

At a Glance ▪ Winner of the National Jewish Book Award, this book tells the story of a Jewish family who escaped from Germany to Switzerland and then to America shortly before the outbreak of World War II. It is appropriate for elementary school readers and some readers at the junior high/middle school level.

Summary ▪ It is 1938 and Lisa Platt and her family are increasingly worried by Nazi treatment of Jews in Germany. Some family members and friends urge them to leave, while others think they should stay. Papa goes to America to secure work and the immigration papers that will allow Lisa, her two sisters, and Mother to go to America also. Meanwhile, they flee to Switzerland, telling Nazi officials they are going for a short vacation. Unable to take goods or very much money with them, they encounter numerous hardships as they await word from Papa that he has permission for them to come to America. Lisa is befriended by a Catholic family who helps her and her family. Finally, they are allowed to go to America.

> My thoughts were jumbled, and I felt a heaviness in my chest. I couldn't help thinking of what Clara had said about Papa, that it took courage for him to leave Germany. For Dr. Michels, the courageous thing was to remain. How strange it was, how difficult to understand, that Rosemarie's father and mine must do exactly the opposite, and that in each case it was right. (p. 31)

Teaching Considerations ▪ Ask your students to imagine that they and their families had to flee from danger like Lisa Platt's family did in *Journey to America*. Tell them: "You are allowed to take only one special thing with you in addition to your basic clothing. What would you take and why?" Good companion books are *Jacob's Rescue* by Malka Drucker and Michael Halperin and *Behind the Secret Window: A Memoir of a Hidden Childhood During World War II* (see chapter 3).

Lowry, Lois. *Number the Stars.*
Houghton Mifflin, 1989; Dell Yearling, 1990. 137 pages.

Then they were there, in front of her. Four armed soldiers. With them, straining at taut leashes, were two large dogs, their eyes glittering, their lips curled. (p. 112)

At a Glance ▪ A 1990 Newbery Award Medal winner, this story is set in Denmark, 1943, and tells how Annemarie Johansen and her family help her best friend, Ellen Rosen, and her family to escape from the Nazis. It is appropriate for readers at the elementary school level, and the age and gender of the main character will not deter either junior high/middle school readers or males from reading this because of the danger and heroism of the story.

Summary ▪ In 1943, Copenhagen is a city under siege with the invading Germans on every corner. Life has remained relatively normal for best friends, ten-year-old Annemarie Johansen and Ellen Rosen, but they are frightened by the soldiers and they miss butter and other foods that are in short supply. They are proud of King Christian X who remains strong, even with Germans in his country. Their normal life ends when the Nazis begin their "relocation" program for the Jews in Denmark. Annemarie's family does not sit idly by; they help Ellen's parents escape to the country and they take Ellen in as their "third daughter." But the challenges for Annemarie are just beginning because she and her family must reunite Ellen with her parents and then help them to escape to neutral Sweden.

"Friends will take care of them," Mama said gently. "That's what friends do." (p. 24)

Teaching Considerations ▪ After reading *Number the Stars,* have the students put themselves in either Annemarie's or Ellen's place in each of the following situations: (1) on the street with the Nazi soldiers; (2) when the Nazi soldiers come to the Johansens's apartment; and (3) at the farmhouse the night the Rosens leave. Give them opportunities to dramatize these events. Excerpts can be read aloud to students from Pettit's *A Place to Hide: True Stories of Holocaust Rescues* as a follow-up (see chapter 3).

Morpurgo, Michael, *Waiting for Anya*. Scholastic, 1990. 172 pages.

"Children," said Widow Horcada sniffing. "Jewish children. He collects them, don't you Benjamin?" Benjamin said nothing. "They get passed down all through France and when they get here he keeps them for a week maybe, sometimes longer, till they're strong enough for the journey; and then he takes them over the mountains into Spain and to safety." (p. 42)

At a Glance ▪ Jo helps a widow and her son-in-law shelter Jewish children in a small French village until they can cross over the mountains to safety. When German troops begin to close off the border, the entire village becomes involved in a plan to save the children. This book is appropriate for elementary school children and will also appeal to junior high/middle school students.

Summary ▪ Jo and his family live in a small village in German-occupied France. While hoping that his father will return soon from the war, Jo is secretly helping an elderly widow and her son-in-law, Benjamin, shelter Jewish children on the outskirts of town until they can cross over the mountains to safety in Spain. Benjamin continually hopes that his daughter, Anya, will be among the arriving children. Jo's family and village seem safe until a small German outpost is established there. But the soldiers seem friendly and the town settles into an uneasy truce with them. Jo even develops a friendship with a German corporal whose daughter is killed in a bombing raid on Berlin. Jo's grandfather discovers his secret and helps the widow and Benjamin as conditions become more precarious for the hidden Jewish children. When Jo's injured father returns from the war, he is angry at what he considers the village and his son's collaboration with the enemy. As the Germans step up their border patrols and become suspicious of the widow, Jo and his family embark upon a dangerous plan involving the entire village to save the children.

Jo turned. Coming out of the trees were three soldiers. Everyone had seen them now. No one moved. No one said a word. There was no doubt about it, the one in front was the Corporal. (p.153)

Teaching Considerations ▪ This book not only tells an exciting story with elements of danger, but also develops some of the many complexities present during wartime. The German soldiers are pictured as real people, some of whom have problems and questions and doubts of their own. Jo's father returns from the war as a angry, moody man who drinks too much. Throughout the story, Jo must make a number of important and difficult decisions. Help your students to identify with Jo and ask what they might have done in similar situations. *A Pocket Full of Seeds* by Marilyn Sachs is a good companion book (see entry in this chapter).

Additional Titles: Elementary School Level

Best Friend by Elisabeth Reuter. (P)

Bridge to Freedom by Isabel R. Marvin. (JM)

Daniel's Story by Carol Matas. (JM)

Devil's Arithmetic by Jane Yolen. (JM)

Hide and Seek by Ida Vos. (JM)

Rose Blanche by Roberto Innocenti. (AL)

Junior High/Middle School Level

Marvin, Isabel R. *Bridge to Freedom.* Jewish Publication Society, 1991. 136 pages. (JM, E)

"You don't understand!" Tears streamed down her face. "They're dead. All of them." Sobs shook her body. "The Nazis have been killing the Jews they took to concentration camps."

He stared at her in amazement. "That's impossible. Rachel—stop! Are you telling me your family was—. No human being would simply put another to death without a trial, without a reason!" (p. 25)

At a Glance ▪ Rachel, a young Jewish girl, and Kurt, a fifteen-year-old deserter from the crumbling German Army, seek escape and freedom in the last days of the war. This book is appropriate for junior high/middle school students and some elementary school students.

Summary ▪ Rachel and Kurt are both escaping; she because she is Jewish and he because he was forced into the army even though he is only fifteen. Kurt stumbles into a cave where he finds Rachel caring for an injured dog, Fritz. By necessity, they become allies. Kurt wants to return to his family's farm and Rachel needs to get to her grandmother and aunt in Belgium. They must find food and avoid capture by the Nazis; Kurt must also avoid American troops who will take him prisoner. They decide that it is safer for both of them to go to Belgium until the war is completely over, but they have a dangerous journey ahead. Kurt makes Rachel promise that if he is caught, she will continue without him.

> Outside the tower, Rachel walked along the bridge walkway, her left hand gripping the leash, her right hand holding the taped wire. Tears mixed with rain streamed down her face. Dawn began to lift the darkness as she reached the west bank.
>
> TO BELGIUM, the road sign read. Belgium—passage to freedom. Or despair. (p. 85)

Teaching Considerations ▪ This book presents a different view of the Holocaust. Help students to address stereotypes by looking at different groups in this book. For some, this book could serve as a good introduction to *Friedrich* by Hans Peter Richter, which tells the story of a friendship between a Jewish and a German boy (see entry in this chapter).

Matas, Carol. *Daniel's Story.*
Scholastic/United States Holocaust Memorial Museum, 1993.
136 pages.

We are alive. We are human, with good and bad in us. That's all we know for sure. We can't create a new species or a new world. That's been done. Now we have to live within those boundaries. What are our choices? We can choose evil like our enemies have done and create a world based on hate. Or we can try to make things better. (p. 70)

At a Glance ▪ Daniel traces his life through the pictures in his family album, until he is without a camera in the camps, and then he takes pictures in his mind of all that he sees.

This book has appeal to a wide range of readers. While it is probably most appropriate for junior high/middle school readers, some elementary school students will enjoy it, especially when used with the video. It also holds the interest of secondary school readers.

Summary ▪ Daniel's family has lived in Germany for over a thousand years and now they are being told that they do not belong there because they are Jews. When his uncle is sent away to a concentration camp, Daniel is given his camera. He is determined to become the "official" family photographer. He takes photos of the family and of family events, but he also photographs the city of Frankfurt as the Nazis take charge. He even wears a Hitler Youth uniform as a disguise so that he can travel freely along the streets and see what is happening. He takes his camera when the family is deported to Lodz Ghetto and there he also records the times.

Later his talent as a photographer is put to use after he is sent to Auschwitz. The Resistance has him take pictures of the inhuman treatment people are experiencing so that there is some documentary evidence of the Nazis' actions. Daniel serves as an assistant to the camp photographer at Buchenwald, photographing the guards and their families in the closing days of the war.

> "It's over Daniel," he said. "It's over."
> And then I realized that he was right. We were free. And alive. I sank down beside him, unable to feel anything but an immense sense of relief. Perhaps happiness would come later. (p. 117)

Teaching Considerations ▪ *Daniel's Story* is based on a composite of young people who lived during the Holocaust and is the focus of an exhibit for children at the United States Holocaust Memorial Museum. A video and resource packet are available (see chapter 7). In *Daniel's Story*, Daniel sees his world through the lens of a camera or through the photographs that he has taken. Have your students imagine that they are with the liberating forces at one of the camps. Have them describe the first three pictures that they would have taken. Biographies and personal narratives that can be used as companions to this book are *At the Heart of the White Rose: Letters and Diaries of Hans and Sophie Scholl* by Inge Jens, which describes the actions of a small resistance group of German students, and *MISCHLING, Second Degree: My Childhood in Nazi Germany* by Ilse Koehn (see chapter 3). Two books written by German author Hans Peter Richter, *Friedrich* and *I Was There*, provide a powerful account of the Nazi madness from the perspective of a German boy growing up during this tragic time (see entries in this chapter). *Camera of My Family: Four Generations in Germany, 1845–1945* is an award-winning film for junior high/middle school and secondary school students (see chapter 7).

Vos, Ida. *Hide and Seek.* Translated by Terese Edelstein and Inez Smidt.
Houghton Mifflin, 1981,1991. 132 pages.

Because we don't want to go to a camp, we hide from the Germans. That is called "being in hiding." We may no longer go outside, and we must be very quiet. No one is supposed to know where we are and no one is supposed to hear us.

I am angry. I am afraid. (unnumbered)

At a Glance ▪ In this award-winning book, Rachel tells the story of her family's life from 1940 to 1945 during the German occupation of Holland; their years in hiding from the Nazis; and their painful adjustments afterwards. It is appropriate for junior high/middle school readers and some elementary school readers.

Summary ▪ Rachel is eight years old in 1940 when the German invade The Netherlands. Life becomes more and more difficult and dangerous as restrictions are placed on Jews, and friends and family members disappear. Eventually, her family must go into hiding to survive. For a time they are able to stay together, but when it becomes too dangerous, Rachel and her younger sister, Esther, must go by themselves to stay with a Christian farm couple. The family is reunited when the war is over in 1945, but then they face the emotional after effects of adjusting to the years of fear, deprivation, and loss.

> Can you imagine how it feels when you find out that people you love are dead, all of a sudden?
> Imagine what it would be like not ever to be allowed to go outside, year after year. Imagine being able to do your shopping only between three and five o'clock.
> Imagine . . . (unnumbered)

Teaching Considerations ▪ Have your students imagine that they are in hiding like Rachel and Esther in *Hide and Seek*. Have them discuss how they will spend their time. Then have them plan a one-week schedule showing what they will do. Remind them that they cannot go outside or make noise or listen to the radio, and there is no television. Have them make a list of all the things they would like to do that they will not be able to do. Use any of the several books by or about Anne Frank and/or any of the personal narratives described in chapter 3 as follow-ups to this book.

Yolen, Jane. *Devil's Arithmetic.*
Viking Penguin, 1988; Puffin Books, 1990. 170 pages.

> Outside, where there should have been a long, windowless hall with dark green numbered doors leading into other apartments, there was a greening field and a lowering sky. The moon hung ripely between two heavy gray clouds. A bird pelted the air with a strange, lilting song. And across the field, stepping in the furrows, marched a shadowy figure. He had a shapeless cap on his head, a hoe over his shoulder, and he was singing:
>
> > Who asked you to be buried alive?
> > You know that no one forced you.
> > You took this madness on yourself.
> >
> > (pp. 20-21)

At a Glance ▪ For Hannah, her grandfather's stories of the Holocaust are ancient history. But when she opens the door for the prophet Elijah at the Passover seder, she is transported to her grandfather's village in the 1940s, and all of his stories become a reality for her. This superb book appeals to a wide range of readers. While probably most appropriate for junior high/middle school readers, some secondary school readers and elementary school readers also will enjoy it.

Summary ▪ Hannah thinks she's having a dream or that her grandfather is playing a game with her when she opens the door of his apartment in the Bronx and walks into the Polish village that her family came from before the Holocaust. Not only is she transported in space, but also in time, because it is shortly before Passover in 1942 and the Nazis have just arrived to take the Jews away. Hannah or Chaya, as she is known in the village by her Hebrew name, is taken away with the rest of the villagers and begins life in the concentration camp. Survival becomes a daily challenge. This book is a recipient of the National Jewish Book Award and the Sidney Taylor Book Award.

> Without thinking through the why of it, Hannah snatched the kerchief off Rivka's head. "Run!" she whispered. "Run to the midden, run to the kitchen. The guard is new. He won't know the difference. One Jew is the same as another to him. Run for your life, Rivka. Run for your future. Run. Run. Run. And remember." (p. 159)

Teaching Considerations ▪ Have the students discuss why they think the author used the technique of time travel in this book and their assessment of its effectiveness. This book can also be used as a springboard to this type of writing. Have your students select an historical event from the Holocaust that interests them and research it. Then write a story in which they (or their characters) are transported to that time. What is it like? How is it different from today? What kinds of things do they see? And any other questions appropriate to their understanding of the period. *Tell Them We Remember: The Story of the Holocaust* by Susan Bachrach provides a good historical overview for this book (see chapter 2).

Additional Titles: Junior High/ Middle School Level

Journey to America by Sonia Levitin. (E)

Lisa's War by Carol Matas. (S)

The Man from the Other Side by Uri Orlev. (S)

Number the Stars by Lois Lowry. (E)

Rose Blanche by Roberto Innocenti. (AL)

Sheltering Rebecca by Mary Baylis-White. (E)

Twenty and Ten by Claire Huchet Bishop. (E)

Waiting for Anya by Michael Morpurgo. (E)

Secondary School Level

Matas, Carol. *Lisa's War.*
Scholastic, 1987. 108 pages.

> Suzanne has just killed a man. Shot in cold blood. Could
> I do the same? I think back to the mission she and I were
> on last week, with Stefan and an older man, Olaf. We
> blew up a shoe factory. About ten blocks from the blast,
> a German patrol car stopped us. (pp. 52-53)

At a Glance ▪ When Denmark is invaded, Lisa and her family decide that they must take action against the Nazis. Lisa and her
brother Stefan join the Resistence to take a stand. This book is appropriate for secondary school readers and some junior high/mid-
dle school readers.

Summary ▪ When the Germans invade Denmark, Lisa and her
family know that as Jews they are in a difficult situation. She soon
realizes that her brother Stefan is involved in some action against
the Nazis. She convinces Stefan to let her help. Even though she is
only thirteen, she begins her activities by distributing underground
newspapers. In the next two years her activities increase as the occupation becomes more difficult. Finally, the Nazis order the deportation of the Jews, but the Resistance has other plans.

> I started to call every Jewish family I know. I tell them
> that the rabbi is going on holiday and that they should
> consider a holiday, too. As soon as possible. They un-
> derstand. Then I start to look in the book for Jewish-
> sounding names and to call them. (p. 77)

Teaching Considerations ▪ Because of Denmark's unique position during the war, there are numerous stories of heroism by its people. Have your students explore more about the Danish people and their role in World War II. *Kris's War* by Matas is the sequel to this book (see entry in this chapter). Students will also enjoy Cowan's *Children of the Resistance* as a follow-up (see chapter 3).

Orlev, Uri. *The Man from the Other Side.* Translated from the Hebrew by Hillel Halkin. Houghton Mifflin, 1989, 1991; Puffin Books, 1995. 186 pages.

> Who in Warsaw, in December 1942, was going to admit that he was Jewish? And yet if he didn't learn to cross himself right, it might cost him his life. (p. 59)

At a Glance ▪ Marek, a fourteen-year-old Catholic boy, helps to hide a Jewish man from the Warsaw Ghetto and then goes with him back into the ghetto to fight during the uprising. Appropriate for secondary school readers and some junior high/middle school readers, this exciting and award-winning book has special appeal for young males.

Summary ▪ This captivating story is made even more so by the fact that it is based on the true experiences of a Polish journalist, now dead, whom Uri Orlev met in Israel when they were both adults. Marek, his mother, and stepfather live outside the Warsaw Ghetto. When Marek becomes fourteen, his stepfather includes him in his clandestine smuggling operations providing food and sometimes weapons to Jews in the ghetto through the underground sewer system. His stepfather claims to be anti-Semitic and says he engages in the smuggling only to make money.

When Marek's mother discovers that Marek has joined two young thugs in stealing from an escapee from the ghetto, she reveals the true identify of his father, who is Jewish. Marek's remorse leads him to befriend another escapee and find him shelter. When the Jews in the ghetto erupt into battle against the Nazis, the man insists on returning to fight. Marek accompanies him and engages in battle until his stepfather rescues him and several Jews. This book is not only an exciting adventure story, but it also helps the reader to understand the complexities and inconsistencies of human nature during wartime. Among the awards it has received are the National Jewish Book Award, the Mildred L. Batchelder Award, and designation as an ALA Best Book for Young Adults.

> But that's what wartime is like: suddenly you find out that everything you've thought about your friends, or your neighbors, or your relatives, is wrong. Anyone at all can inform on you or get you into hot water, because when someone is frightened, or hungry, or desperate for money, he's no longer the same person. (p. 10)

Teaching Considerations ▪ Have your students put themselves in the place of Marek in *The Man from the Other Side*. Marek had a number of choices in this book; sometimes he made good decisions, sometimes bad ones. Have the students list the choices Marek had and the decisions he made. Have them discuss which ones they agree with and why, and which ones they disagree with and why. Orlev's award-winning book, *The Island on Bird Street*, a powerful novel about survival in the Warsaw Ghetto, makes an excellent follow-up to this book. Other sources of information about the Warsaw Ghetto are Israel Gutman's book, *Resistance: The Warsaw Ghetto Uprising* (see chapter 2) and the documentary, *The Warsaw Ghetto* (see chapter 7).

Additional Titles: Secondary School Level

Daniel's Story by Carol Matas. (JM)

Devil's Arithmetic by Jane Yolen. (JM)

Rose Blanche by Roberto Innocenti. (AL)

Further Reading for All Levels

Ackerman, Karen. Illustrated by Elizabeth Sayles. *The Night Crossing*. Knopf, 1994. 58 pages. (E, P)

This is a touching story of how a Jewish family escaped Nazi terror by fleeing to Switzerland. Although it is short and simple, the action and drama keep the interest of readers. It can be used as an effective introduction to the Holocaust for those children with little or no background.

Dillon, Eilis. *Children of Bach*. Charles Scribner's Sons, 1992. 164 pages. (JM, S, E)

Peter, Pali, and Suzy return home from school to find their apartment door open and their parents and aunt missing. The Nazis have imprisoned the Jews in Budapest, including their parents, famous Hungarian violinists who were preparing for a large concert that evening. The children try to carry on, making sure that they continue to practice their music every day for as their father had said, "Music and painting and books are the only things that lift people above the animals and make them able to feel the presence of God. No matter what comes next, there will always be music" (p. 12). Their aunt returns and with the help of some Italian neighbors, they escape to a small mountain village in Italy.

Hartman, Evert. *War Without Friends*. Translated from the Dutch by Patricia Crampton. Crown, 1979, 1982. 218 pages. (S, JM)

Fourteen-year-old Arnold's father is a fanatical supporter of the Nazis and a member of the Dutch National Socialist Party. Under his influence, Arnold becomes a member of the Hitler Youth in his small Dutch town. He is scorned and isolated by his classmates, who think he is a German informer. Caught between these forces, Arnold must wrestle with the increasing uneasiness of his conscience and decide what to do.

Keneally, Thomas. *Schindler's List, A Novel*. Simon & Schuster, 1982. 398 pages. (S)

Based on the true story of Oskar Schindler, Keneally's novel uses the testimonies of survivors to portray the actions of a supposed Nazi sympathizer who, through wile and cunning, bribery and courage, cheated the Nazis by rescuing more Jews than any other single individual. Schindler set up factories that employed Jewish workers and kept them from the gas chambers of the concentration camps. See chapter 7 for information on how to obtain the Steven Spielberg film, *Schindler's List*.

Kerr, Judith. *When Hitler Stole Pink Rabbit*. Coward, McCann & Geoghegan, 1971. Dell Yearling, 1987. 191 pages. (JM)

Anna and her family are driven out of Nazi Germany. They begin an odyssey that will take them to a number of European countries in search of refuge from Hitler's men. In spite of the hardships they encounter, the family is true to its resolve to stay together.

Laird, Christa. *Shadow of the Wall*. Greenwillow, 1989. 144 pages. (JM, S)

Misha, age fourteen, and his two younger sisters live in the Orphans' Home run by Dr. Janusz Korczak in the Warsaw Ghetto. Misha smuggles in food to try to keep his sick mother alive; his father has already died in the ghetto of typhus. As conditions deteriorate, Misha smuggles out his youngest sister, a baby, to a safe home that Dr. Korczak has found. When his mother dies and the Nazis deport Dr. Korczak and the children, including his sister, to Treblinka, Misha joins the resistance movement.

Matas, Carol. *Kris's War*. Formerly titled *Code Name Kris*. Charles Scribner's Sons,1989; Scholastic 1992. 152 pages. (S, JM)

This book is a sequel to Matas's book, *Lisa's War*. Kris is the name Jesper, Lisa's boyfriend, uses in the Danish Resistance. He has maintained his friendship with Lisa and her brother, Stefan, as they continue their efforts for the Resistance against the Nazis. Stefen and Jesper were involved with the underground, sabotaging the Nazis and publishing an underground newspaper. Jesper is captured by the Nazis and imprisoned. He is sentenced to be executed, but as he awaits his fate, he reflects on the circumstances that have landed him there. As Jesper faces death, Stefan decides to try to rescue his old friend.

Mazer, Harry. *The Last Mission*. Dell, 1979. 188 pages. (S)

Jack Raab is a large, fifteen-year-old Jewish boy living in the Bronx with dreams of fighting Hitler and becoming a hero in World War II. Using his brother's I.D. and fabricating a story, he joins the U.S. Air Force. After flight training, Jack is sent to England where he and his crew make many successful bombing missions over German-occupied Europe, except for the last one. Shot down, he is sent to a German POW camp. This book has special appeal for male readers.

Orgel, Doris. *The Devil in Vienna*. Dial Press, 1978. 246 pages. (JM, S)

Thirteen-year-old Inge is Jewish and lives in Vienna in 1938. She and Lieselotte have been best friends for a long time, but when

Lieselotte joins the Hitler Youth at the insistence of her father, their friendship becomes complicated and even dangerous. The author, Doris Orgel, uses diary entries and letters based on her own experiences to tell the story of two girls whose friendship endures and grows under extremely difficult circumstances.

Orlev, Uri. *The Island on Bird Street.* Translated from the Hebrew by Hillel Halkin. Houghton Mifflin, 1981, 1983. 162 pages. (S, JM)

An award-winning book, this is a story of ingenuity and bravery as eleven-year-old Alex must survive on his own in the Warsaw Ghetto while waiting for his father to return. As the cold winter months slowly drag on, Alex's situation becomes even more desperate. He must not only battle for physical survival, but he must also battle fear and loneliness. The author, Uri Orlev, was born in Warsaw in 1931 and spent 1939–41 hiding in the ghetto with his mother and young brother. After his mother was killed by the Nazis, he and his brother were sent to Bergen-Belsen.

Ray, Karen. *To Cross a Line.* Orchard Books, 1994. 154 pages. (JM, E)

Egon flaunts the German directive that Jews are not allowed to have drivers' licenses. He drives a motor scooter to make deliveries in his work as a baker's assistant. He is involved in an accident that changes his life because he must flee his native Germany. He then undergoes difficult and dangerous attempts to escape. The book is most appropriate for junior high/middle school students, but some elementary students might enjoy Egon's challenges.

Richter, Hans Peter. *Friedrich* . Translated by Edite Kroll. Holt, Rinehart and Winston, 1970; Puffin Books, 1987. 149 pages. (S, JM)

Winner of the Mildred L. Batchelder Award, this is the story of a Jewish German boy, Friedrich, and his best friend, an Ayran German boy, growing up together in Germany from 1925 to 1942. Told from the first-person perspective of his friend, *Friedrich* is a powerful and moving account of how the persecution of Jews affected ordinary families. Although the reading level is fairly easy, the issues involved are complex. This book is most appropriate for secondary school students and some junior high/middle school students.

Richter, Hans Peter. *I Was There*. Translated by Edite Kroll. Holt, Rinehart and Winston, 1972; Puffin Books, 1987. 204 pages. (S, JM)

Three German boys, each in his own way, are caught up in the turmoil and power of the Third Reich. For different reasons, they join the Hitler Youth movement as young boys and then, as teenagers, the infantry. This book is a first-person account of daily events and attitudes from 1933 to 1943; the author states, "I am reporting how I lived through that time and what I saw—no more. I was there. I believed—and I will never believe again." A powerful book, it could be used effectively with *All Quiet on the Western Front* by Erich Maria Remarque. While the reading level is relatively easy, the issues are complex; therefore, this book is probably most appropriate for secondary school students and some junior high/middle school students.

Sachs, Marilyn. Illustrated by Ben Stahl. *A Pocket Full of Seeds*. Doubleday, 1973; Puffin Books, 1994. 137 pages. (E, JM)

Nicole Nieman and her family live in a small village in France. Nicole is concerned with the typical things of growing up until the Nazis occupy France and her life is changed. Soon their apartment is full of Jewish refugees and discussions about escaping to safety in Switzerland. Nicole returns from school one afternoon to discover that her parents have been taken away. Nicole must hide in order to survive. This book is based on a true story.

Serraillier, Ian. *Escape from Warsaw*. Original title: *The Silver Sword*. Scholastic, 1962, 1972. 218 pages. (S, JM)

Joseph Balicki, his Swiss wife, and three children—Ruth, thirteen; Edek, eleven; and Bronia, three—live in a suburb of Warsaw where Joseph is the headmaster of a school. Arrested by the Nazis in 1940, he escapes and returns to his family only to find his house destroyed, his wife arrested, and his children missing. Based on actual accounts, this story tells how the children stayed together and endured incredible hardships until they were reunited with their parents in Switzerland after the war.

Shemin, Margaretha. Illustrated by Peter Spier.*The Little Riders.* Coward, McCann & Geoghegan, 1963; G. P. Putnam's Sons, 1988; Beech Tree, 1993. 76 pages (E)

Johanna, an American, is visiting her grandparents in Holland when World War II begins. Not only is she far from home and her parents, but her grandparents' village is occupied and a German officer comes to stay in their house. Her grandfather takes care of the local church and one of his special duties is to care for twelve metal figures of noblemen on horseback who adorn the clock tower. The figures, six on each side, ride out from behind two doors as the clock strikes the hour and the bell tower carillon plays Dutch folk songs. Johanna, like her father before her, loves the little riders. When the Nazis decide to take the riders, it is up to her grandfather to hide them. The Nazis are enraged and they take Johanna's grandparents into headquarters for questioning. Johanna must find a way to hide the riders where the Nazis cannot find them.

Treseder, Terry Walton. Illustrated by Lloyd Bloom. *Hear O Israel: A Story of the Warsaw Ghetto.* Atheneum, 1990. 41 pages. (E, JM)

This is a story of a family of Polish Jews, from their experiences in the Warsaw Ghetto until they were taken away to Treblinka. Isaac and his family are devout, but their lives become increasingly difficult in the ghetto. His grandfather collapses and dies, his mother dies in childbirth, the baby does not survive, and another brother and sister die of typhus, but the family keeps its faith. Since food is scarce, the family looks forward to leaving the ghetto to go to a work camp, but their fate is set at Treblinka.

Wild, Margaret, and Julie Vivas. *Let the Celebrations BEGIN!* Orchard Books, 1991. 32 pages. (P)

The young children who survived concentration camps were robbed of the traditional comforts and joys of childhood. This book relates the effort of a group of women imprisoned in Belsen to make toys for all the children who were held there. One of the children, Miriam, remembers her family and her home as she eagerly helps the women collect scraps and buttons to make stuffed animals for the young children who have forgotten family and home. Miriam and the women plan to give the toys to the children at the first party that they will have after the liberation.

Literature Involvement:
Suggestions and Issues for Responding and Thinking

Reading historical fiction about the Holocaust is often a powerful experience for young people. They need opportunities to reflect upon what they are learning and to express their feelings. They also need opportunities to clarify misconceptions and to seek additional information. The following suggestions can be selected according to their appropriateness for the various age groups and then used to provide these opportunities:

- Select one of the characters that you have read about and then imagine what he or she was doing in 1955, 1965, 1975, 1985, and today.

- A message that is repeated throughout the books is the desire of the characters not to let themselves retaliate in kind for their treatment. What is meant by the belief that there is victory in not being like your oppressors?

- *Number the Stars, Lisa's War,* and *Kris's War* all take place in Denmark. What influence does the setting have on the events in these books that makes them different from books set in other countries, such as Poland or Germany?

- A purpose of historical fiction is to instruct and to reinforce values. Select your favorite novel about the Holocaust. Identify and make a list of the major values that are presented in the book.

- Select one value from the listing that you have previously done. Select sentences and phrases from the book to support the significance of that value in the story. (In a classroom setting, students can write their sentences and phrases on the chalkboard or on paper strips to display on the walls. They can then be used to prompt group discussion and as a springboard for writing.)

- Imagine that you are Kris in *Kris's War*, Daniel in *Daniel's Story*, Ellen in *Number the Stars*, or Alex in *The Island on Bird Street*. Write journal entries for seven days explaining your life as it is during the war.

- Design a collage that represents the life of one of the characters you have read about from the books recommended in this chapter.

- Select an incident from one of the books you have read . Dramatize that incident either by yourself or with other members of the class.

5

We Recreate Through Drama

Plays

A total of thirty-five million individuals, civilian and military,
were killed in World War II. The Holocaust of World War II
is frequently thought of as the "Jewish Holocaust." While
the Jews as a people, solely because of their religion, were
singled out for destruction and Six Million perished, five
million non-Jews were also annihilated in the death camps.
These non-Jewish victims included Jehovah's Witnesses,
gypsies, Social Democrats, labor leaders, theologians,
atheists, and ordinary citizens who rose up to protest and
to fight against the Nazis. In addition to those who were
murdered, untold numbers were physically and emotionally
incapacitated because of the horrors and deprivations they
experienced. Millions more suffered the dangers and
traumas of escape and the rebuilding of their lives in
alien countries.

Ina R. Friedman, *Escape or Die*

The numbers of the Holocaust are staggering and the massiveness
of the destruction in some ways dulls the horror. Plays, however,
have the innate ability to put human faces to acts of conflict, terror,
suffering, hope, love, and bravery. Through characters and stories,
the spectrum of human emotions and behaviors is communicated.

Dramatic literature and performance make real those lives, saved or lost, irrevocably ordered by history. Plays make immediate and actual the situations of the Holocaust, bringing intimacy, empathy, and involvement to our knowledge of it.

In this chapter are plays of people, real and fictional, whose personal stories *are* the stories of the Holocaust. Content is not confined to a particular time, place, or religious group. These scripts are about the young, the old, the imprisoned, the doomed, and the free. They are about the persecutors and the victims. Some of the characters, like Anne Frank, lived and are now famous. Others are fictional and have been created in endeavors to share and to understand through the art of theatre.

Various genres, from tragedy to satire, are represented, and all age groups, relationships, and long-term psychological and emotional effects are portrayed. In examining the Holocaust through dramatic literature, we gain insight into the human condition. Through drama, we see the people, hear their words, know their hearts, and connect their experiences to our own.

Prior to Reading: Think About . . .

A play is different from other forms of literature in that it is created to be performed rather than read. Further, while one gathers in a particular place and with others in order to be a member of an audience, viewing a play is still a rather private and personal matter between actors and individual audience members. Being a cast member and working on developing a character, or contributing to the collective and collaborative nature of play production as another theatre artist, such as a playwright or designer, brings additional dimensions to the theatre experience. In order to explore drama in performance, dramatic imagination, and dramatic literature with students, the following questions can be used to stimulate thinking:

- How is a play different from a story in a book? When a story is adapted for the stage, what changes might occur?

- Some of the plays in this chapter have been inspired by true events or adapted from other media. How have they been changed to suit the stage?

- What is the difference between drama and theatre?

- How is narration handled in dramatic literature? How is time compressed? How are characters and dialogue used to tell a story?

- What is involved in bringing a story to life on the stage? What are the responsibilities of various theatre artists (actors; directors; costume, scenic, lighting, and sound designers; and playwrights) in the theatrical process?

- What differences are there between reading a play, either silently or aloud, and seeing it performed?

- The most essential relationship in the theatre is that between audience member and actor. Further, drama is immediate and engages the audience member on both emotional and intellectual levels. How do these characteristics influence audience response to plays about the Holocaust?

- Given the power of a play to create lasting and strong impressions, why is it important to discuss scripts and performances of Holocaust plays?

- The more one knows about the playwright, historical period, and cultural climate in which the play is set or was written, the richer the dramatic experience is likely to be. What kind of research might be undertaken to better understand the plays in this chapter?

Focus: We Recreate Through Drama

Auschwitz by Peter Barnes. In *Plays of the Holocaust,* edited by Elinor Fuchs. (S)

Broken Glass by Arthur Miller. (S)

The Diary of Anne Frank by Frances Goodrich and Albert Hackett. (AL)

Good by C. P. Taylor. (S)

Hitler's Childhood by Niklas Rädström. Translated by Frank Gabriel Perry. (JM, S)

I Love You, I Love You Not by Wendy Kesselman. (JM)

Incident at Vichy by Arthur Miller. (S)

I Never Saw Another Butterfly by Celeste Raspanti. (E)

I Never Saw Another Butterfly by Celeste Raspanti. (JM, S)

The Man in the Glass Booth by Robert Shaw. (S)

Mister Fugue or *Earth Sick* by Liliane Atlan. In *Plays of the Holocaust,* edited by Elinor Fuchs. (S)

Playing for Time by Arthur Miller. (JM, S)

Remember My Name by Joanna Halpert Kraus. (E)

Shadows of the Holocaust: Plays, Readings and Program Resources by Harriet Steinhorn and Edith Lowy. (E, JM)

A Shayna Maidel by Barbara Lebow. (JM, S)

Shoorik and Poufchik by Flora B. Atkin. (P)

Two by Ron Elisha. (S)

The Young Guard by Anatoly Aleksin. (JM, S)

All School Levels

Goodrich, Frances, and Albert Hackett. *The Diary of Anne Frank.* Random House, 1956. 174 pages.

> ANNE: (*going to him*) I know it's terrible, trying to have any faith . . . when people are doing such horrible . . . But you know what I sometimes think? I think the world may be going through a phase, the way I was with Mother. It'll pass, maybe not for hundreds of years, but some day . . . I still believe, in spite of everything, that people are really good at heart. (p. 168)

At a Glance ▪ This is, quite possibly, the best known Holocaust play. Based upon the diary of young Anne, it chronicles her experiences as she and her family hide from the Nazis in a cramped attic space above a warehouse. The diary ends with Anne's capture by the Gestapo, but the play assures that her spirit will live eternally.

Summary ▪ Anne Frank, the members of her family, and several other people hid from the Nazis for more than two years. The play presents the details of that existence. It captured the Pulitzer Prize, the Antoinette Perry Award, and the Critics' Circle Award as much for its rich characterizations as for its obviously engrossing plot. Anne Frank is an alert, spirited, intelligent, and emotionally captivating adolescent. Through her, the reader encounters the terror of Nazi domination and the hope of liberation. When the family is finally located and Anne goes to her death, it is clear that a forgiving and aspiring individual has been lost.

> ANNE'S VOICE: And so it seems our stay here is over. They are waiting for us now. They've allowed us five minutes to get our things. We can each take a bag and whatever it will hold of clothing. Nothing else. So, dear Diary, that means I must leave you behind. Good-bye for a while. P.S. Please, please, Miep, or Mr. Kraler, or anyone else. If you should find this diary, will you please keep it safe for me, because some day I hope . . . (p. 171)

Teaching Considerations ▪ As a writing exercise, ask the students to keep a diary for recording their activities and thoughts. As they complete study of the play, ask them to compare and contrast their entries to Anne's. You might also have them write to the Anne Frank Center and request related materials. Study of the play can be further supplemented with films or videos about Anne Frank (see chapter 7).

Primary School Level

Atkin, Flora B. *Shoorik and Poufchik.*
Unpublished. Available from the playwright (contact through the American Alliance for Theatre and Education), 1982. 14 pages.

> SHOORIK: No, no, don't break it. Keep it and give it to some other boy who will win the competition. But don't

break it . . . Don't break it! Where are you taking me? I have to tell my grandfather goodbye. Stop pushing me. I promised grandpa. I would play a last piece on my violin for him before we leave. (p. 6)

At a Glance ▪ A puppet play suitable for nine- and ten-year-olds but possible to use with younger children, *Shoorik and Poufchik* reflects the Jewish experiences of persecution and resettlement. While not a Holocaust play, it reminds the reader that it is still difficult to practice Judaism in some parts of the world.

Summary ▪ Eight-year-old Shoorik and his mother, Russian *refusniks,* are finally able to leave Russia and settle in New York. The play shows the youngster's early experiences in America and contrasts his life here with that in his homeland. Youngsters will identify with his school encounters and with his love for his dog, Poufchik.

JUDY: He ran away from the pogroms. They tried to kill all the Jews. (p. 13)

Teaching Considerations ▪ Ask students how many of them have pets and why pets are important to people. Discuss moving and adjusting to a new home. Ask children to compare Shoorik's life in Russia to his life in the United States.

Additional Plays: Primary School Level

The Diary of Anne Frank by Frances Goodrich and Albert Hackett. (AL)

Elementary School Level

Kraus, Joanna Halpert. *Remember My Name.* Samuel French, 1989. 128 pages.

MARIE-THÉRÈSE: Many people have died for France. You, Madeleine, must live for France. (p. 86)

At a Glance ▪ Ten-year-old Rachel Simon is sent, alone, to St. Laurent des Pins when the Germans take over Marseilles. Her courage, and the courage of those who help her, is the focus of the play.

Summary ▪ When the Germans occupy Marseilles, Rachel Simon's parents send her to the Haute-Loire region in Auvergne in south central France where they hope the young Jewish girl, using a false name, will be safe. There she finds protection with a priest, a war widow, and members of the Underground. Each of these characters, in his or her own way, combats the atrocities of the Nazis. The play centers upon their courageous and humane responses which ultimately reunite Rachel and her father.

> RACHEL: It's over, Papa. The war's over. We can stop hiding! I can have my name back. My own name. RACHEL SIMON! (p. 110)

Teaching Considerations ▪ Ask the students to imagine that they have to escape from their hometowns and assume false identities elsewhere. Ask them to write autobiographies for their newly invented personæ. Share these orally.

Steinhorn, Harriet, and Edith Lowy. *Shadows of the Holocaust—Now and Then*. In *Shadows of the Holocaust: Plays, Readings and Program Resources*. Kar-Ben Copies, 1983. 80 pages.

> MRS. SOLOMON: Nazi soldiers searched the street outside the ghettos. They inspected trolley cars and trains. They demanded identification. Those who couldn't prove that they were not Jewish were tortured and beaten until they confessed. Sometimes mistakes were made, and Christians were accused of being Jewish and were tortured. (*Shadows of the Holocaust—Now and Then*, p. 35)

At a Glance ▪ This collection of short plays and other resources is specifically intended to help today's child better understand the Holocaust. The collection includes five plays, ranging in length from eight pages to two brief acts. It is also appropriate for junior high/middle school levels.

Summary ▪ Each of these plays, in some way, chronicles the Jewish experience at the hands of the Nazis. All require minimal staging and are specifically intended for use in educational settings. Plots center around such topics as desiring to return to the ghetto, helping a friend to escape the concentration camp, and being forced to leave a sick parent. Each play is noteworthy for its simple and straightforward dialogue and characterization. The focus of the plays is to make important historical and emotional content more comprehensible to youngsters.

> LISA: Every time I hear children play, or see them walking in the street, I turn to them in the hope that maybe it's my little brother or sisters. Even though I was told they all died in Poland, I still can't accept it. (*The Letter*, p. 51)

Teaching Considerations ▪ Encourage students to read personal narratives of or to conduct interviews with Holocaust survivors. Students might also be asked to improvisationally create scenes based upon what they would experience if they were German Jews during the Nazi reign of terror.

Additional Plays: Elementary School Level

The Diary of Anne Frank by Frances Goodrich and Albert Hackett. (AL)

I Never Saw Another Butterfly by Celeste Raspanti. One-act play. (JM)

Junior High/Middle School Level

Aleksin, Anatoly. *The Young Guard*. Translated by Miriam Morton. New Plays, 1977. 80 pages.

> KLER: Fanatics! . . . Execute them? Shoot them? . . . No . . . That's too light a punishment! Into the coal pit with them! Down the shaft! The coal pit! And the coal trolleys down on top of them! The coal trolleys! . . . (p. 79)

At a Glance ▪ The dramatic conflict is a psychological battle between the Fascist interrogator, Kler, and members of the youth resistance movement, The Young Guard. Episodes of interrogation are interspersed with scenes that chronicle the actions and relationships of the adolescents in this underground organization. The play is also appropriate for the high school level.

Plays

Summary ▪ During the war, a network of teenagers organizes a resistance network in Krasnodon, near Stalingrad. They engage in activities that include freeing Soviet prisoners of war, burning Nazi headquarters, and destroying German supplies. The play shows the activities, interrogation, torture, and murder of the young freedom fighters. It is a psychological battle orchestrated through flashback and vignette. The actions and themes of the play contrast logic and illogic, despair and hope, as well as survival and sacrifice.

> ULYANA (*with anger and despair*): I despise you! Yes, I despise your helplessness, your tears. There is so much grief all around us—so many healthy, strong, wonderful people are dying at the front, in torture chambers— imagine how their wives, their mothers suffer. But every-one works, struggles! And you . . . you are offered help and you whine, and even want to be pitied. I don't pity you. No, I don't! (*After a pause*) Valya! Valiuchka, what good friends we were! My little heart! (*Valya sobs.*) Think back—did I ever give you bad advice? Valiuchka! I implore you! (p. 66)

Teaching Considerations ▪ Several interesting activities are recom-mended in conjunction with the study of this play. One simple task is for the students to learn the song, "Where Are You Flying Bird So Free," as it appears in the script. Another is to create a bulletin board of trouble spots around the world where students believe young freedom fighters might be working for their causes. As a writing activity, students could identify a cause for which they would risk their lives and describe why this cause is so important to them. They might also read the novel, *The Young Guard*, and compare it to the play. As this script largely presents a psychologi-cal conflict, students might discuss this type of struggle and identify films or plays they have seen which employ it.

Lebow, Barbara. *A Shayna Maidel.* NAL Penguin, 1988. 94 pages.

> LUSIA: Stop! I don't want to hear! We can't be like them! We can't do what they did! And I don't want a warm coat. I want to be cold like the dead ones. I don't want— (p. 63)

At a Glance ▪ The play is about a family that has been separated, and some members lost, during the Holocaust. They are reunited in the United States, but the war has affected each one in a deeply personal way. The play is also appropriate for the secondary school level. Yiddish expressions are explained in a glossary at the end of the play.

Summary ▪ Rose has been raised in the United States after fleeing Poland with her father and has become completely "Americanized." Her mother and sister stayed behind. In the play, Rose's sister, Lusia, is finally reunited with her family in New York. The war, however, has created emotional voids and losses for each member of the family and they must struggle to once again be relatives who can truly communicate with one another.

> ROSE: I was only four when we left. It's so strange that you have memories of me, that I was part of your life. That I was born in another world. I don't remember any of it. Just a feeling, maybe. Sometimes there's a particular smell when something's cooking or a song comes on the radio and all of a sudden I feel different, like I'm in another place. (p. 24)

Teaching Considerations ▪ This play can be a springboard for discussion of family structure and communication. It can also be the basis for discussing how students would react if their family structures were altered. As a research project, ask students to investigate incidents where siblings have been raised apart from one another and to report their findings.

Kesselman, Wendy. *I Love You, I Love You Not.* Samuel French, 1988. 57 pages.

> DAISY: Are you sure you're Jewish? You're really a Jew? You certainly don't seem it. You certainly don't look it. (*She pauses.*) Jew, Jew. What is it about that word, Nana? Animal. Vegetable. Mineral. Jew. How can they tell? Can they smell one? But not you, Daisy. Not ever you. We love you, Daisy. We'll always love you. (*Looking out.*) Except for the eyes. That's the one thing that gives it away. But maybe—if I keep the sadness out of my eyes—maybe I'll be safe. Maybe they won't find me.

They won't recognize me. Maybe they won't take me away. (*She pauses.*) I don't want to be chosen, Nana. (p. 48)

At a Glance ▪ The play focuses upon Daisy, an adolescent, and her relationship with her grandmother, Nana. Daisy's grandmother has been in a concentration camp, and both characters in this play are, in their own ways, survivors. (Please note: This play contains some explicit language.)

Summary ▪ Daisy and Nana have a loving, although not always an easy, alliance. Daisy's relationship with her parents is apparently dysfunctional, making her visits with Nana even more intimate and special. Nana, however, is a Holocaust survivor, and by watching as she and Daisy interact, we are able to see how fears, insecurities, caring, trust, love, dependency, and loss affect families throughout generations.

> NANA: You were so tiny. Not even three. "What's that?" you said. (*Imitating Daisy at three.*) "What's that, Nana?" *(She laughs softly.)* And month after month, year after year went by, and it was always, "Nana, what is that? Why do you wear that? Why do you have that on your arm?" (*She pauses.*) And then one day, I was putting some dishes up on the shelf, when I felt those huge eyes staring at me. And I heard, "Nana—"

> DAISY: (*Breaking in. Slowly.*) "Are you sure you didn't do anything wrong to make them do that to you?" (*She leans closer and touches Nana's arm. Quietly reading the number out loud.*) "A. A is for Auschwitz." (p. 51)

Teaching Considerations ▪ This play is an excellent vehicle for examining meaningful family relationships. Students might, for example, identify why a particular family member is a special person to them. It also stimulates discussion of family and intergenerational communication. In conjunction with study of the play, you might consider inviting a Holocaust survivor to visit the class and talk about how experiences during the Holocaust have affected his or her family. Students may wish to create family trees and display them in the classroom.

Miller, Arthur. *Playing for Time.*
Dramatic Publishing Company, 1985. 91 pages.

ESTHER: They don't want it to seem like it's a war to save the Jews. (*All turn to her.*) They won't risk planes for our sake, and pilots . . .their people wouldn't like it. (*To Fania*) Fania . . . if they do come for us, and it's the end . . . I ask you not to do that again and beg for your life. (p. 80)

At a Glance ▪ This is a full-length theatrical adaptation of Fania Fenelon's book and Miller's earlier television film. It is the story of Fenelon's experience as a member of a women's orchestra in a concentration camp. The play is also appropriate for the secondary school level.

Summary ▪ Fania Fenelon's selection to be a member of a female orchestra in the concentration camp saves her life and the lives of other musicians who form this group. Their experiences, will to survive, and the dismal and horrifying conditions in which they exist, make this a compelling play.

FANIA (*quietly, simply, painting a picture*): They'd been so horribly beaten they could hardly stand. But Mala refused the executioner's help and stayed on her feet under the noose. The whole camp, thousands of people, were made to watch. And suddenly, as the two of them were dropped and swung from the ropes, someone in the crowd removed his cap. Then another did, and slowly a sea of shaven heads was bared. The SS clubbed at them, ordered them to cover up, but very few obeyed and they gave up clubbing, there were so many. Edek I'd never seen, but Mala was so beautiful . . . Alma'd been right, she was a miracle. They hung there in the rain all afternoon. Even in the dark they let them hang there . . . to show their contempt for us all . . . for life, I suppose. (*There is a blackout.*) (pp. 76–77)

Teaching Considerations ▪ Compare the book, television film, and play. Stage scenes from the play in the classroom. If students play instruments, have them form a classroom orchestra.

**Rädström, Niklas. *Hitler's Childhood*. Translated by
Frank Gabriel Perry.
Folmer Hansen Teaterförlag AB, n.d. 93 pages.**

FATHER: I know . . . I know that I have to be a hard
taskmaster, a harsh disciplinarian. Being hard is something I have to take upon myself. I have to be cruel. We
have to learn to be cruel with a good conscience. The
strong have the right before God and the whole world
to impose their will. Adi, we have to force ourselves into
greatness, if we are to fulfill our duties, take our rightful
place in history. Harshness is the sacrifice I make. Are
you listening? (p. 69)

At a Glance ▪ The play imagines Hitler's early years, vividly illustrating abuse in a dysfunctional family. It projects the impact of this
upbringing on his later life.

Summary ▪ The infamy of the adult Hitler is well known. One
rarely, however, thinks of the childhood that may have shaped the
adult. In the play, abuses suffered at the hands of his domineering
father, the mental and emotional deficiencies of his mother and
aunt, and Hitler's psychological mechanisms for coping with his
family, present a challenging study in personality development. The
social and historical implications resulting from this child abuse
and later manifestations of invisible scars are traced through this
troubling family portrait. Students will find the psychological dimensions of the play particularly engrossing.

ADOLF: You're falling down into the darkness now and
I'm the one who pushed you. You were standing at the
very edge and the blind women who led you there had
already returned to their cocoons. I've broken the steps
to bits and burnt up the rope. You're falling now. I'll
stamp on your hands when they try to catch hold of the
grass. I'll keep kicking you in the face till no one will
want to say your name any more. And while you're falling, I'll have kept a part of you back and tied it to a
tree-root and when you're falling, you'll unwind out of
yourself and you'll hang down into the darkness like a
bloody rope down into the abyss. And at the very bot-
tom of the rope your tongue will be fluttering, trying to

say the name of all the children, but that's when I'll cut it off. (p. 89)

Teaching Considerations ▪ The play opens with actors asking audience members questions. The following are included:

> FIRST ACTOR: Adolf Hitler was one of the greatest mass murderers who ever lived. Can you imagine Hitler as a young boy or a little child? When did he become Adolf Hitler? How does a child grow up to be a monster? Perhaps we are born evil? (p. 1)

Discuss these questions. What others could you ask your students? Can correlations be drawn between Hitler and other mass murderers? What are these parallels?

Raspanti, Celeste. *I Never Saw Another Butterfly.* Dramatic Publishing Company, 1971. 35 pages.

> RAJA: One by one the transports came. Mother, Father, Aunt Vera—they went. Pavel and Irca—they went. Everyone I knew and loved in Prague. There was no one who could remember me before I had come here as a child of twelve . . . but there were many left standing at the train as the transports started up, the cars crowded, boarded, sealed . . . (p. 19)

At a Glance ▪ This is a one-act version of the full-length memory play described in the following entry. It is also appropriate for the elementary level. The one-act version is sometimes used for forensic contests by older students.

Summary ▪ See following entry for summary.

> RAJA: Mother, Father, Pavel, Irca. I hear you. Honza, I hear and I remember . . . Irena Synkova, I remember. (*She picks up the sack and adjusts her coat. She pushes up the sleeve of the coat and looks at a number on her arm, then determinedly, pulls down her sleeve. She faces the audience again.*) My name is Raja—I am a Jew; I survived Terezin—*not* alone, and *not* afraid. (p. 33)

Teaching Considerations ▪ With students, discuss relationships that are important to them. Ask them to share memories of important events. Compare the one-act version of the play to the full-length script.

**Raspanti, Celeste. _I Never Saw Another Butterfly._
Dramatic Publishing Company, 1971. 51 pages.**

RAJA: I never saw another butterfly. . . .
The last, the very last,
   so richly, brightly, dazzling yellow.
Perhaps if the sun's tears sing
   against a white stone . . .
Such, such a yellow
Is carried lightly 'way up high.
It went away I'm sure because it
   wished to kiss the world goodbye.
For seven weeks I've lived in here,
Penned up inside this ghetto,
But I have found my people here.
The dandelions call to me,
And the white chestnut candles in the court.
I never saw another butterfly.
That butterfly was the last one.
Butterflies don't live in the ghetto.
                                    (pp. 22–23)

At a Glance ▪ The play is a memory play, told from Raja's point of view, of her years as a child in Terezin. Of her family and friends, only she survived the Holocaust. It is appropriate for junior high/middle school and secondary school levels.

Summary ▪ Raja is taken to Terezin as a child and grows to womanhood there. Through her memories, her account unfolds of the progression of terror in Prague, the loss of her family and friends, the importance of her secret schooling, her first romantic stirrings, her life in Terezin, and her relationship with her beloved teacher, Irena. While the story is filled with sorrow, it is ultimately one of courage. Raja's fate is not Auschwitz. She is liberated and returns to Prague, alone but alive.

RAJA: Fear—this is half the story of Terezin—its beginning, but not its end. I was a child there, I knew that word. I became a woman there because I learned another word from Irca and Pavel, from Father and Mother, from Irena Synkova. I learned the word "courage" and found the determination to live—to believe in life . . . (p. 30)

Teaching Considerations ▪ Please see suggestions for the one-act version of the play, cited earlier in this chapter. With older students, discuss the concept of a memory play. Tennessee Williams's masterpiece, *The Glass Menagerie*, is an example they might know. Can they identify other such works? If they were to create a memory play, what personal recollection might be the basis of the work? Discuss with them the notion that memory is selective. How might this influence a playwright?

Additional Plays: Junior High/ Middle School Level

The Diary of Anne Frank by Frances Goodrich and Albert Hackett. (AL)

Shadows of the Holocaust: Plays, Readings and Program Resources by Harriet Steinhorn and Edith Lowy. (E)

Secondary School Level

Atlan, Liliane. *Mister Fugue or Earth Sick.* In *Plays of the Holocaust,* edited by Elinor Fuchs. Theatre Communication Group, 1987. 51 pages.

MISTER FUGUE: No. Not necessarily. War or no war, at the end they put us in the earth and it's the earth you can't escape, whether you die in bed or in a valley! What counts is to have done something before that, whether or not it does any good. Let's do something. Here. (p. 68)

At a Glance ▪ Mister Fugue is a runaway German soldier who forsakes his duties so that he might accompany a group of Jewish ghetto children to a camp and, ultimately, to their deaths.

Plays 121

Summary ▪ Atlan's central character was inspired by Janusz Korczak, the Polish-Jewish physician who accompanied the children from his orphanage to the death camp at Auschwitz. "Fugue" translates to "flight" or "escapade" in French, the playwright's native language. The flight detailed in the play is one of imagination, as Mister Fugue and the four children he befriends tell stories and invent games which reflect the milestones of life. These five characters do not survive and the play leaves the reader to ponder if the message of their destruction is one of final hopelessness or renewal and rebirth.

> GROL: Once upon a time, there was a soldier. He would have wanted to lead them to the forest, but the children hadn't followed, he could have lied to them, but he didn't, the proof, he got in the back of the truck, they'll kill him in the Rotburg valley. (p. 61)

Teaching Considerations ▪ Research Janusz Korczak. Discuss how this real person has inspired the playwright. Identify other examples of real people being fictionalized in drama.

Barnes, Peter. *Auschwitz*. In *Plays of the Holocaust,* edited by Elinor Fuchs. Theatre Communication Group, 1987. 42 pages.

> GOTTLEB: That's where I should be too. Out in the field. Not stuck behind a desk in Orienburg, but in the gas chambers of Auschwitz, working with people. Dealing with flesh and blood, not deadly abstractions: I'm suffocating in this limbo of paper. Auschwitz is where it's happening, where we exterminate the carrion hordes of racial maggots. I'd come into my own there on the Auschwitz ramp, making the only decision that matters, who lives, who dies. You're young, live; you're pretty, live; you're too old, too weak, too young, too ugly. Die. Die. Die. Die. Smoke in the chimneys, ten thousand a week. (p. 135)

At a Glance ▪ The play is a dark comedy with graphic imagery and explicit language which uses the format of the music hall to illustrate the bureaucracy of the Third Reich.

Summary ▪ English playwright Peter Barnes has penned a black farce and, in so doing, makes a point about complacency and the horror of the Holocaust. His characters are the bureaucrats of Hitler's Germany. Barnes encourages laughter at their unending rules, regulations, paperwork, and fear of protest, and at their meaningless lives. In the end, however, as the horror of Auschwitz is chillingly revealed, the laughter turns to disgust. Recognition comes that, while these lives may be banal, at least they are ongoing while for those whom these bureaucrats process, Auschwitz is an end of existence.

> GOTTLEB: We need more plants like Auschwitz, manufacturing and recycling dead Jews into fertilizing ash. We've already reached a peak output of 34,000 dead gassed and burned in one day and night shift. A record Belsen, Buchenwald, Dachau or Treblinka can't touch. And it's all due to the new gas chambers and crematoriums. You help build 'em so you should be able to see 'em plain. They've been made up to look like public bath houses. "Our Wash and Steam'll Help You Dream." The dressing rooms've signs in every European language, "Beware of Pickpockets," "Tie Your Shoes Together and Fold Your Clothes," "The Management Takes No Responsibility for Any Losses Incurred." Oh we're clever, we're clever. Don't you see how clever? It helps calm those marked down to die as they go naked along carpeted passages to the communal washroom. Fifteen hundred a time. (p. 137)

Teaching Considerations ▪ Study the format of music hall entertainment. Have the class create a show based upon this format and present it to others in your school. Or, taking a more serious direction, identify and analyze characteristics of comic genres. Discuss how and why Barnes uses comedy to treat the decidedly serious subject of the Holocaust.

Elisha, Ron. *Two.*
Dramatic Publishing Company, 1990. 83 pages.

> CHAIM: What would you know! . . . My genteel little gentile. (*He turns away.*) . . . What would you know?

. . . (*Pause.*) It's true that, after the war, I could walk into any shop in town, brandish my tattoo, and march heedlessly to the head of the queue . . . And the half-starved Germans, mute in their guilt, just stood there . . . Sometimes, I didn't even have to pay! . . . But, the world being what it is, the effect soon began to wear off. The tattoo, however, did not. (p. 37)

At a Glance ▪ This two-character play offers a philosophical discussion of good and evil as Chaim, the rabbi, gives Anna, the former SS member, Hebrew lessons so that she might leave Germany for Palestine.

Summary ▪ In 1948, shortly after the end of World War II and the official declaration of the existence of the Jewish state, Anna enlists Chaim, a rabbi who has survived the concentration camp, as a Hebrew teacher. She believes that knowledge of the language will help her to make a new life for herself in Palestine. The lessons, however, yield both linguistic and philosophical insights as the Hebrew alphabet becomes the vehicle through which good and evil are discussed. During the lessons, each character engages in more self-disclosure. Chaim, once the religious leader, has become an atheist, while Anna forsook her Jewish roots to become a member of the SS. Their relationship becomes one of renewal as they help each other to heal emotionally.

ANNA (*passionate*): Rav Chaim Levi—there *are* no "others"! . . . Jew and Arab. Victim and executioner. Saint and Devil . . . They are *us* . . . There *are* no others. Rav Chaim Levi—you *know* these things, but you don't live them. You see yourself as the "other," so you try to shut yourself off from the rest of the world. But you can't. Because a rabbi living in Germany *is* a German. And a Jew is part of Palestine simply because there *are* Jews in Palestine. And to suggest that a member of the SS is not a human being is every bit as dangerous as the suggestion that a *Jew* is not a human being. To accept that good is a part of being human but that evil is not is to suggest that none of us is human. It is a short step from that suggestion to the gates of Auschwitz. (p. 74)

Teaching Considerations ▪ Using maps and newspaper articles, trace the historical development of Palestine. As this is still a troubled area of the world, create a chart or matrix upon which issues and positions of various factions can be visually displayed. After engaging in this type of study, students can stage a classroom version of a news interview show, casting classmates as representatives of the principal parties. Another option is to identify and discuss the philosophical issues raised in the play.

Miller, Arthur. *Broken Glass.*
Penguin Books, 1994. 98 pages.

> SYLVIA: But it's in the paper—they're smashing up the Jewish stores . . . should I not read the paper? The streets are covered with broken glass! (p. 109)

At a Glance ▪ The Gellburgs look like a successful and happy New York couple until Sylvia develops hysterical paralysis. As their lives are examined, it seems that destructive events in Germany parallel and contribute to the despair that Sylvia and Phillip privately experience. The play contains sexually explicit material.

Summary ▪ In New York in 1938, Phillip Gellburg is a successful Jew in a gentile firm. His wife suffers from hysterical paralysis which seems to be related to political events in Germany. Doctors can find nothing physically wrong with her. The Gellburgs present a public facade of success while their private lives deteriorate. Their marriage and their lives are studies in despair. The broken glass of the title symbolizes the smashing of storefronts of Jewish merchants in Germany, the glass broken that is a part of the Jewish wedding ceremony, and mirrors used for inner reflection.

> GELLBURG: . . . I want you to tell her—tell her I'm going to change. She has no right to be so frightened. Of me or anything else. They will never destroy us. When the last Jew dies the light of the world will go out. She has to understand that—those Germans are shooting at the sun! (p. 174)

Teaching Considerations ▪ Discuss the use of symbolism in drama. Focus upon the symbolism in the play. Research and share findings related to the image of broken glass and the Jewish experience.

Miller, Arthur. *Incident at Vichy.*
Dramatist Play Service, 1964. 54 pages.

MONCEAU: I beg your pardon. The Russians condemn the Jews and the middle class, the English have condemned the Irish, Africans, and anybody else they could lay their hands on; the French, the Italians . . . every nation has condemned somebody because of his race; look at the Americans and what they do to Negroes. The vast majority of mankind is condemned because of its race. What do you advise all these people—suicide? (p. 38)

At a Glance ▪ Six men and a fifteen-year-old boy are interrogated at a detention center in Vichy, France in 1942. Each knows that unless released or able to escape, he could become a victim of Nazi terror. Explicit language.

Summary ▪ The play can be staged in a metaphoric or realistic manner. In either format, the critical element is Von Berg's emerging sense of responsibility. Although a detainee, his background will earn his freedom. He comes to recognize, however, that although he has not been a part of Nazi terrorism, he shares in responsibility for it. The play is a philosophical presentation in which the responsibilities and abilities of the individual to make a difference are scrutinized.

BAYARD: The cars are locked on the outside. (*Slight pause.*) And they stink. You can smell the stench a hundred yards away. Babies are crying inside. You can hear them. And women. They don't lock in volunteers like that. I never heard of it. *(A long pause.)* (p. 16)

Teaching Considerations ▪ This play promotes examination of the concept that one person can make a difference. Discuss with students the merit of that idea and ask them to support their opinions. Follow this with actual cases students find where, they believe, one person's efforts have resulted in something significant.

Shaw, Robert. *The Man in the Glass Booth.*
Samuel French, 1968. 67 pages.

GOLDMAN: (*Rises to her.*) Always call a spade a spade. Those euphemisms you speak of were best for keepin' order—they didn't want the typists to get the message—you follow? But in my case I'm not here to tell you I didn't enjoy it—I'm here to tell you I did. (*Goldman laughs.*) No clerk, Rosen! Issued my own orders, plotted my own plots, had a ball. You follow? (p. 35)

At a Glance ▪ Arthur Goldman lives the life of a successful financier in Manhattan until his arrest as a Nazi war criminal. The play presents a portrait of Goldman before and during his trial. Explicit language.

Summary ▪ The play is a suspenseful and harsh look at a suspected Nazi criminal's life in America, subsequent arrest for war crimes, and trial in Israel. Shaw's drama presents a disturbing picture of human behavior. Arthur Goldman's wealthy and respected lifestyle is in sharp contrast to the actions of which he is accused.

GOLDMAN: Yes, I remember that, but *you* did great—remarkable constitution. Course, some of you might be wonderin' why Mrs. Levi and her head friends got on the train in the first place—got on the train to the quarry. There was only three guards, as I recall—Kirlewanger's got a villa in Cairo, I'm here, and Pohse's drawing a pension in Hamburg—anyway, why did all those people keep gettin' on cattle trains and goin' to quarries and suchlike? Might I enlighten you on that, Your Honor? (p. 49)

Teaching Considerations ▪ In conjunction with this play, study the hunt for suspected Nazis and Nazi war crimes trials. There have been reported sightings and, several years ago in Ohio, the arrest, trial, and deportation of a suspected Nazi war criminal. Stage a mock war crimes trial in your classroom.

Taylor, C.P. *Good.*
Methuen, 1982. 97 pages.

HITLER: And I promise you, I will never give you an order which goes against your conscience. (p. 39)

At a Glance ▪ John Halder is a German professor who slowly becomes immersed in Nazi politics. The play shows how a "good" man could rationalize his own actions, even when they bring destruction to others. Explicit language.

Summary ▪ John Halder, at the start of the play, is a rather apolitical German professor of literature. As the action progresses, he becomes more deeply involved in the Nazi party, all the while rationalizing his own behavior and continuing to believe that he is a good man. The only questioning he engages in comes in the form of musical pieces he hears in his head. The play juxtaposes Halder's reality with musical counterpoint. By the play's end, he has become a high-ranking official at Auschwitz, illustrating the extent of his moral decline.

> HALDER (*to himself*): I love Jews. I'm attracted to their whole culture. Their existence is a joy to me. Why have they got to be a bloody problem to everyone? (*To Maurice:*) You know that, Maurice . . . Nobody takes that metaphysical racialist rubbish in *Mein Kampf* seriously. . . . Pure races and foul, perverted, spiritually-riddled-with-disease Jews . . . Nobody can even *read* it! (p. 63)

Teaching Considerations ▪ Use this play to explore the moral and psychological justifications used by Nazis during the Holocaust. Extend the learning experience by examining contemporary atrocities around the world and discussing how perpetrators might justify their actions.

Additional Plays: Secondary School Level

The Diary of Anne Frank by Frances Goodrich and Albert Hackett. (AL)

Hitler's Childhood by Niklas Rädström. (JM)

I Never Saw Another Butterfly by Celeste Raspanti. (JM)

A Shayna Maidel by Barbara Lebow. (JM)

The Young Guard by Anatoly Aleksin. (JM)

Further Reading for All Levels

Fuchs, Elinor, ed. *Plays of the Holocaust: An International Anthology.* Theatre Communications Group, 1987. 310 pages. (S)

Plays in this anthology are *Eli: A Mystery of the Sufferings of Israel* by Nelly Sachs, translated by Christopher Holme; *Mister Fugue* or *Earth Sick* by Liliane Atlan, translated by Marguerite Feitlowitz; *Auschwitz* by Peter Barnes; *Replika* by Józef Szajna, translated by E. J. Czerwinski; *Ghetto* by Joshua Sobol, adapted by Jack Viertel; and *Cathedral of Ice* by James Schevill. These plays represent the international perspective of the collection. Additionally, there is an excellent appendix directing the reader to numerous plays. Listings for *Eli* and *Replika* follow.

Futterman, Enid.*Yours, Anne.* (JM)

Contact the Empire State Institute for the Performing Arts (Albany, NY, Tel. 518-443-5222) for information about this musical version of *The Diary of Anne Frank.* An excellent resource workbook is available upon request.

Mauro, Robert. *Children of the Holocaust.* Meriwether, 1989. (S)

This can be performed as a play, reader's theatre performance, or radio drama. The concept is one of teenage victims of the Holocaust speaking from the grave.

Sachs, Nelly. *Eli: A Mystery Play of the Sufferings of Israel,* translated by Christopher Holme. In *Plays of the Holocaust,* edited by Elinor Fuchs. Theatre Communications Group, 1987. 53 pages. (S)

Sachs, a 1966 co-winner of the Nobel Prize for Literature, wrote *Eli* three years after her 1940 escape from Berlin. The play is a surrealistic quest as the shoemaker, Michael, searches for Eli's killer. Young Eli was murdered as he asked God for help and as his parents were being led away to their deaths. Sachs envisions a healing for the Jewish community in a play influenced by myth, folk ritual, and dance.

Sherman, Martin. *Bent.* Avon Books, 1979. 68 pages. (S)

This play treats the Nazi persecution of homosexuals and chronicles the character of Max as he goes from a normal life to flight, arrest, imprisonment in a concentration camp, and, ultimately suicide. His homosexual relationships and, finally, awareness of love are revealed in this play that treats a subject of Nazi atrocity less frequently discussed than the murder of Jews.

Skloot, Robert, ed. *The Theatre of the Holocaust: Four Plays.* University of Wisconsin Press, 1982. 333 pages. (S)

Plays in this anthology are *Resort 76* by Shimon Wincelberg, *Throne of Straw* by Harold and Edith Lieberman, *The Cannibals* by George Tabori, and *Who Will Carry the Word?* by Charlotte Delbo.

Solway, Kenneth. *Son/My Son.* Unpublished. Presented in conjunction with the Holocaust Museum Awareness Project. Available from The Kogod Chapel, Adas Israel Synagogue, Washington, D.C. 13 pages. (S)

The play shows the effect of the Holocaust on the character of a father who has lost his first-born son to the Nazis. He has sired a second son, but he is haunted by his loss and his parenting responses are undeniably influenced by his fear and anguish.

Szajna, Józef. *Replika.* Translated by E. J. Czerwinski. In *Plays of the Holocaust,* edited by Elinor Fuchs. Theatre Communications Group, 1987. 6 pages. (S)

Replika is a performance piece rather than a play. It evolved from an art installation in the Venice Biennale, 1970, and centers around the rebuilding of a civilization that has been annihilated as a result of some future event of destruction. Out of the attempt to rebuild, however, emerges a monster who must ultimately be destroyed. Szajna's performers can create a replica but cannot reproduce an authentic new world. The piece can be construed as a warning to mankind about world devastation. It is recommended only for those older students who can appreciate the concept of a performance piece and is not recommended for those requiring a structured script.

Literature Involvement: Suggestions and Issues for Responding and Thinking

Reading plays about the Holocaust is often a powerful experience for young people. They need opportunities to reflect upon what they are learning and to express their feelings. They also need opportunities to clarify misconceptions and to seek additional information. Plays encourage visualization of events and empathy with characters. They can serve as catalysts for forming meanings as well as inducements for further study. The following suggestions can be selected according to their appropriateness for the various age groups and then used to provide these opportunities.

- Compare/contrast the scripted version of one of the plays you have read with a stage performance of the same play. What are the similarities? What are the differences?

- Perform staged readings in your classroom of scenes from plays in this text. How does the emotional impact of the scene change when dialogue is read aloud?

- In creating a character, an actor or actress will often research the time and place in which the character lived, delve into the background of the playwright to see how his or her personal experiences have influenced the writing, learn the customs and manners that would be natural for that character, and create autobiographical sketches for the person portrayed. Select a character from a play that you have read and do each of these things for that character.

- Select a monologue or scene from one of the plays you have read. Perform this for your classmates. To extend the learning experience, you should memorize the lines, stage the movements, and set the stage using available furniture and props. Costume the character and incorporate the hairstyles and make-up of the period. After the performance, share with classmates what you have learned about theatrical elements and the production process.

- Discuss how theatre happens. What is the role of the director? Designers? Actors? Playwright? Why is the actor/audience relationship essential to the theatrical process?

6

It Must Not Happen Again

Fiction, Nonfiction

> And still the lesson the Holocaust has to teach us has not
> been learned. Prejudice, bigotry, and hatred have not
> disappeared. On the contrary, in the past few years violent
> acts motivated by prejudice have increased. And often the
> people guilty of painting swastikas on Jewish buildings, of
> attacking Jews, blacks, and others, are young people.
>
> David A. Adler, *We Remember the Holocaust*

While the Holocaust officially ended at the end of World War II, its aftermath has lasting repercussions. This chapter examines literature that reflects ongoing concerns about humanity and the treatment of Jews. The historical context of bias and persecution against Jews created a society that tolerated or looked the other way, allowing the systematic destruction to occur. This chapter presents an historical perspective through fiction and nonfiction which shows that the struggles the Jews endured did not end with the war. Fiction and nonfiction related to the hardships they endured, including the difficulties of making new homes after the war, is discussed; also explored is contemporary fiction that reflects the continuing impact of the Holocaust and nonfiction that documents the attitudes and activities of hate groups today.

Certainly a number of groups have suffered persecution throughout time and in virtually every culture; however, for the purposes of this book and this chapter we are focusing on the events of the Holocaust and its aftermath. The events of World War II reflect inhuman treatment of many people, including Allied prisoners of war at the hands of both the Germans and the Japanese, and the incarceration of Japanese-Americans in detention camps throughout the western United States. Abuses continue: in Bosnia as documented in *Zlata's Diary;* in Haiti as shown in *A Taste of Salt: A Story of Modern Haiti;* in the stories of conflicts in African nations; and in Central and South America.

While all of these events present a tragic perspective on massive social injustices, there has never been a systematic attempt to destroy a group of people of the magnitude of the Holocaust. It was the first widespread act of genocide sanctioned as official governmental policy by an industrialized nation that had long been a center of education, the arts, and scientific success. The enemies of the Third Reich were not slaughtered in battles or in random acts. Many of the best scientific and medical minds were charged with creating the methods and facilities to enact a policy of assembly-line annihilation. Even more chilling than the official policy was the public complicity. In a political environment where human life was being systematically destroyed, citizens chose to look the other way and ignore the criminality that was a daily reality. Perhaps this general public indifference is the most alarming lesson of the Holocaust. While Gypsies, political opponents, prisoners of war, and others also perished at the hands of the Nazis, no group was victimized as badly as European Jews. Only as we remember and honor these victims of the Holocaust do we take the first step toward ensuring that atrocities of that magnitude never happen again.

Prior to Reading: Think About . . .

Reading fiction and nonfiction related to contemporary times and issues can be a tremendous influence in helping young people learn about the Holocaust. It affords them with opportunities to explore how ongoing prejudice and discrimination affect their lives and the lives of others. Youthful readers can identify with these events and think about their consequences today. The following questions can be used to prompt this discussion:

- How do you think Holocaust survivors deal with their experiences?

- What would it be like to be the only member of your family to survive?

- Why do some people persecute others? What causes prejudice?

- How do well-meaning people inadvertently contribute to prejudice?

- Cite examples of biased behavior that you have either witnessed or heard about.

- Identify hate groups in the United States. Who are they and who are their targets?

- What do hate group philosophies have in common with the beliefs of Nazism?

- Do you think we could ever have another Holocaust?

- Choose a book from the following titles and read the quotes from it. What do you think they mean? What do you think they reveal about the story?

Focus: It Must Not Happen Again

Chernowitz! by Fran Arrick. (JM, S)

David and Jonathan by Cynthia Voigt. (S)

Gavriel and Jamal. Two Boys of Jerusalem by Brent Ashabranner. Photographs by Paul Conklin. (E, JM)

Gentlehands by M. E. Kerr. (S, JM)

Grace in the Wilderness: After the Liberation 1945–48 by Aranka Siegal. (JM, S)

The Mozart Season by Virginia Euwer Wolff. (JM, S)

The Old Brown Suitcase: A Teenager's Story of War and Peace
by Lillian Boraks-Nemetz. (S, JM)

Skinhead by Jay Bennett. (S, JM)

The Tattooed Torah by Marvell Ginsburg. (P, E)

Terrible Things by Eve Bunting. (AL)

To Life by Ruth Minsky Sender. (IM, S)

Tunes for Bears to Dance to by Robert Cormier. (JM, S)

All School Levels

Bunting, Eve. *Terrible Things.*
Harper and Row, 1980. 25 pages.

"But why did the Terrible Things take them away?"
Little Rabbit asked. "Do the Terrible Things want the
clearing for themselves?"

"No. They have their own place," Big Rabbit said.
"But the Terrible Things don't need a reason. Just mind
your own business, Little Rabbit. We don't want them
to get mad at us." (p. 12)

At a Glance ▪ In this deceptively simple picture book, Eve Bunting
dramatically demonstrates the importance of people sticking together. This book is appropriate for all ages.

Summary ▪ Eve Bunting's parable uses the creatures in a forest
clearing by a pond to personify the Nazis' imprisonment of their
political enemies, people with impairments, and those from ethnic
groups that they disliked. The peaceful world of the clearing is disrupted by the menace of the Terrible Things who come first to take
away all the birds. The other creatures remain mum and even rationalize that the birds were "too noisy." And that is just the beginning.

"Nonsense," Big Rabbit said. "Why should we
move? This has always been our home. And the Terrible
Things won't come back. We are the White Rabbits. It
couldn't happen to us." (p.19)

Teaching Considerations ▪ *Terrible Things* is a powerful book that can be used effectively with all ages. Read the book aloud initially and let the students discuss what they think it means. Help them to see any parallels with life today. Then help them to see the parallels with Nazism and the Holocaust. The film/video, *Hangman*, could be used with older students (see chapter 7). Also with older students, share the following words of Pastor Martin Niemoeller and help them to discuss the parallels between his thoughts and this book.

> In Germany, the Nazis first came for the Communists and I didn't speak up because I wasn't a Communist. Then they came for the Jews, and I didn't speak up because I was not a Jew. Then they came for the trade unionists and I didn't speak up because I was not a trade unionist. Then they came for the Catholics and I was a Protestant so I didn't speak up. Then they came for me: by that time there was no one left to speak up.

Note: There are several variations of this statement attributed to Martin Niemoeller. This one was taken from Philip Friedman's *Their Brothers' Keepers*, p. 100.

Primary School Level

Ginsburg, Marvell. Illustrated by Martin Lemelman.
The Tattooed Torah.
UAHC Press. 1983, 1994. 25 pages. (P, E)

An evil man, Adolf Hitler, had started a war. His Nazi soldiers marched into Brno, Czechoslovakia, Little Torah's city. The Nazis closed all the synagogues. They ordered that all the Torahs, mantles, and other religious items be sent to the city of Prague. (unnumbered)

At a Glance ▪ Set in contemporary times, this is the story of an American looking for a Torah small enough for his son to handle during services. He finds a Torah taken by the Nazis from a synagogue during World War II. This picture book can be read aloud to primary school children and is also appropriate for elementary school children.

Summary ▪ This is the story of a small Torah that is stolen by the Nazis along with hundreds of other Torahs and put in the Michle Synagogue in Prague, which they converted into a warehouse. The Nazis had identification numbers put on all the stolen Torahs, an affront because it defaced the sacred Torahs. The numbering was like the tattoos that the Nazis put on Jewish arms in the concentration camps. The book traces the travels of the Torah from its home in a Brno synagogue to its storage in Prague. After the war, the Torah remains in storage until an American finds it as he looks for a little Torah for his son to carry for services.

> Back home, Mr. Weil had a red velvet mantle made especially to fit Little Torah. The mantle was decorated with a gold Jewish star and the word *Zachor* (Remember). (unnumbered)

Teaching Considerations ▪ The author calls the numbering of the Torahs "tattooing" to parallel the tattooing of Jews and others in Nazi concentration camps. This book can be used with *The Number on My Grandfather's Arm* (see chapter 2) as a springboard for a discussion on the dangers in labeling people. Help students to empathize with people who are singled out for exclusion.

Additional Books: Primary School Level

Terrible Things by Eve Bunting. (AL)

Elementary School Level

Ashabranner, Brent. Photographs by Paul Conklin.
Gavriel and Jamal: Two Boys of Jerusalem.
Dodd, Mead, 1994. 94 pages.

But there is a difference that casts its ever-present shadow over both boys, over the Middle East, and over the rest of the world that cannot help but be involved. The difference is this: Gavriel lives his life as a young citizen of a proud new nation called Israel. For Jamal, a homeland—a country Palestinians can call their own—remains somewhere in the future. (p.16)

At a Glance ▪ This book presents a photographic biography of two boys living within a mile of each other in Jerusalem, but one is Jewish and the other is Palestinian. The book is appropriate for elementary or junior high school/middle school students.

Summary ▪ This is an account of the lives of two boys who are close in age: Gavriel is twelve and Jamal is fourteen. While their lives are quite similar in many ways, there is a significant difference: Gavriel is Jewish and Jamal is an Arab. For all that they have in common, they have a history that divides them. The parallel stories of their lives and families speaks to the difficult political situation. The book provides an excellent insight into both cultures.

> Gavriel and Jamal have never met. It is probable that they have passed each other in the crowded streets of the Old City or have seen each other playing on the Old City walls, but it is quite unlikely that they will ever get to know each other. The gulf between the Jewish quarter and the Arab quarter is wide. (p. 88)

Teaching Considerations ▪ Use a map to show students where Jerusalem is and how small it is. Articles from newpapers and magazines can be used to help students see what life is like in Jerusalem. Have them discuss what it would be like to live in a divided city. Use a Venn diagram (overlapping circles) to depict the similarities and differences in these two boys' lives.

Additional Books: Elementary School Level

The Tattooed Torah by Marvell Ginsburg. (P)

Terrible Things by Eve Bunting. (AL)

Junior High/Middle School Level

**Arrick, Fran. *Chernowitz!*
Bradbury Press, 1981; Signet, 1983. 188 pages.**

> I know they must have been in the back of my mind somewhere, about how mindless bigotry is . . . and hatred . . . and how much energy it takes.

Emmett had the energy to hate a lot. He needed to hate me. Or someone. I'm Jewish, but if I were black or gay or a member of any other minority, it would have been the same. (p. viii)

At a Glance ▪ When Bobby Cherno enters high school, his life become difficult. He is the target of the class bully, who torments him throughout the ninth grade and the summer because he is a Jew. When tenth grade starts and Emmett continues his reign of abuse, Bobby knows it is time to take action. While the message is appropriate for high school as well as middle school/junior high school students, the age of the protagonist may deter some high school students from reading it.

Summary ▪ *Chernowitz!* is a classic among books for young adults. Its frank yet sensitive approach to prejudice makes it a riveting experience. This story of bigotry and cruelty is a powerful one with a message that everyone can learn from. Throughout the ninth grade Emmett Sundback vents his anger and viciousness on Bobby Cherno, harassing him because he is Jewish. He makes threats and keeps Bobby generally miserable. Bobby's friends, fearful that they will become targets of Sundback, go along with the harassment, leaving Bobby alone, betrayed, and isolated. Bobby keeps most of the problem to himself, believing that he should handle it without his parents' help. After a year, the stakes escalate when Emmett tries to kill the Chernos's cat. For Bobby, this is the turning point. He knows that he cannot win in a physical battle with Emmett, but he also knows that he can out-think and out-plot the slow-witted bully. Bobby plans and executes the perfect revenge, but then he must wrestle with his own conscience.

> I didn't feel good and couldn't feel good. Not only about Sundback getting his, but about anything. I kept going over it and over it in my head. I had really taken it all year from Sundback, and not just me, Bob Cherno, but Jews in general with me as their representative. Sundback deserved to be punished for that; it's like games: there are rules for playing games and there are rules for living life, and one of the rules is you don't hate people for their race or color or religion or anything like that. And if you do hate somebody because of their race or

color or religion, then you're not allowed to do anything to them, like persecute them in any way. It's in the Constitution, it's why the Pilgrims came here, it's a rule, it's a law. (p.155)

Teaching Considerations ▪ The childhood chant incorrectly says ". . . and words can never hurt me." Help your students to recognize the power of language to shape how individuals see themselves and their world. Help them to see the impact of adolescent name-calling and stereotyping as a means of bantering with their peers. Have the students develop a code of language to live by in your class. Cormier's book, *Tunes for Bears to Dance to,* and *CityKids Speak on Prejudice* from the CityKids Foundation make good companion books (see entries in this chapter).

Cormier, Robert. *Tunes for Bears to Dance to.* Delacorte, 1992. 101 pages.

Mr. Hairston's favorite pastime was standing at the window near the big brass cash register, watching people passing by on the street, and making comments about them.

"Look at him, Selsky. A kike. Charges too high for his goods. Always running a sale but jacking up the prices before the sale, then coming down a little . . ."

Or:

"There goes Mrs. O'Brien. An Irisher. Nine kids. Spends most of her time in bed. But not sleeping . . ."

Or:

"Look at her, Mrs. Karminski . . . Sloppy," Mr. Hairston said. "Too much rouge on. Pampers that dog. Pays good money for dog food. Leaves her house and lets her slip show. Dumb. A Polack." (p. 5)

At a Glance ▪ In this powerful but brief novel, Robert Cormier explores prejudice and its evil implications. In typical Cormier fashion, human nature is revealed without any attempt to sugarcoat reality. Although the protagonist is young, this book could be used with both high school or middle school students.

Summary ▪ Henry's family is in disarray. His brother Eddie has died, leaving his parents racked with grief. Henry's father is so grief-stricken that he can't work. The family has moved to a new town because the parents can't deal with the memories in their old home. Henry's life is influenced by two men: an old man who befriends him and the owner of the grocery store where he works. The old man is a Holocaust survivor and his employer is a bigot and racist. Henry is caught between these two and he is forced to make major decisions.

> Astonished, Henry thought:
> *It was me he was after all the time. Not just the old man and his village. He didn't want me to be good anymore.*
> (p. 94)

Teaching Considerations ▪ This book presents the age-old struggle between good and evil. Help your students examine the decision-making that Henry goes through. Have them suggest other courses of action and their possible ramifications. *Chernowitz!* by Fran Arrick is a good companion book. See chapter 7 for films/videos by survivors that will help students to more fully understand the experiences of the old man in the book who is a Holocaust survivor.

Sender, Ruth Minsky. *To Life*.
Macmillan, 1988; Puffin Books, 1990. 229 pages.

> We have no time for a long courtship. We need no long courtship. We need each other. An urgent, burning need to rise from the ashes, to build again, fills our hearts and minds. We are alone. No family to share our joy, to tell us mazel tov, congratulations. (p.48)

At a Glance ▪ In *To Life,* Ruth Minsky Sender continues the story of her life following the liberation of the Nazi labor camp at Grafenort that began in *The Cage* (see chapter 3).

Summary ▪ Some people have the impression that when the war ended, survivors returned home and picked up the pieces of their lives, but that wasn't true in most cases. For many Jews everything they had had was destroyed in the war—there were no homes to go back to. Families were separated and survivors didn't know the fate of their relatives. And so it was for Riva. While her imprisonment is over, Riva's struggles are not. She is threatened by Polish vigilantes who continue to murder Jews after the war is over. She never has enough food. Yet, Riva is determined to find any family that is left. This book traces her struggles for the five years following the war, her marriage, her reunion with a few members of her family, the birth of her first two children, and their immigration to the United States.

> My heart pounded as I stared at the letter before me. It is an official letter concerning our immigration to America. Moniek and I are requested to appear for an interview with an American official. (p. 189)

Teaching Considerations ▪ Help your students to understand the period following World War II by having them do research on relocation camps. What options were open for those who had been in these camps? Which countries welcomed refugees? Where did help for them come from? In addition to reading Sender's other books, students may want to read other accounts of survivors (see chapter 3). *Alicia, My Story* by Alicia Appleman-Jurman is an appropriate companion book for older readers and tells of her postwar experiences (see chapter 3).

Siegal, Aranka. *Grace in the Wilderness: After the Liberation 1945–48.* Farrar, Straus, & Giroux, 1985; Puffin Books,1994. 220 pages.

> Then Iboya's voice split the waiting hush in the room. I had to make her repeat what she said before I dared accept it. "Etu is alive! Our sister Etu is alive!" (p. 72)

At a Glance ▪ In this sequel to *Upon the Head of the Goat: A Childhood in Hungary 1939–1944* (see the entry in chapter 3), Piri and Iboya have survived their time in Bergen-Belsen. Now they must try to rebuild their lives.

Summary ▪ In the days following World War II, Piri and Iboya want to go home, but they don't have a home to return to. They have a difficult time as they try to find a home. They search for members of their family and finally they do hear from their sister Etu, who has married and left for Palestine. They end up in Sweden, where they are treated kindly by a couple named Rantzow who offer them a home. But they have decisions to make. Piri falls in love with Erik, but she knows it will not work out because she and Iboya have a dream to be reunited with their relatives. They plan and dream about going to the United States where their remaining relatives live.

The focus was on the future; I was the kid sister who had some maturing to do. "The family was kind, remarkable, to take in and care so much about a Jewish child; they are to be commended," I heard Mrs. Slobodkin repeatedly telling her friends about the Rantzows. (p. 217)

Teaching Considerations ▪ Change is difficult under any circumstances, but for survivors of the Holocaust, it presents special problems. Piri was forced to make a number of significant decisions in her life. Ask your students to select one of the decisions and speculate what might have happened if she had chosen differently. Then have them compare her experiences with those of Riva in *To Life* or Annie in *The Journey Back* or Anna in *Anna Is Still Here* (each of these books is described in this chapter).

Wolff, Virginia Euwer. *The Mozart Season.* Henry Holt, 1991; Scholastic, 1993. p. 249.

She looked at me for quite a while with her intense eyes. "Allegra, here's something about doing music— or painting a picture or anything. When you're doing it, you have to remember everything you've ever learned, and simultaneously forget all of it and do something totally new." She was silent for a while more. "Because if you do the first part and not the second, you're making music or art just like everybody else's. It's not your own." (p. 58)

At a Glance ▪ Allegra Shapiro is a gifted violinist who is preparing for a major musical competition in which she will be the youngest competitor to play Mozart's Fourth Violin Concerto. Although the protagonist is only twelve, this book is probably most appropriate for high school students because she is quite precocious.

Summary ▪ In preparing for a major violin competition, Allegra Shapiro must learn how to look within herself to find the meaning of her music. As she practices, and seeks a way to release her understanding of and feeling for the Mozart Fourth Violin Concerto, she also wrestles with her family history as she learns about her great grandmother who perished at Treblinka. Allegra is surrounded by a number of interesting and supportive adults who nurture her.

> I held the purse against my stomach.
> My great-grandmother. Elter Bubbe Leah.
> Dead at Treblinka.
> I felt a homesickness. For what? Something I'd never seen. I didn't even know what it was. Bubbe Raisa was inviting me to be something—forcing me to be something nobody else had ever even mentioned. I didn't know how to be it. All I knew was that there was a homesickness. I stared at the purse on my arm in the mirror. (p. 172)

Teaching Considerations ▪ Allegra displays her determination to accomplish something that is difficult but very important to her. Have students compare her determination with experiences of their own or with other people they have read about. This book is replete with vivid minor characters. Have students select a minor character that they felt was effective and have them explain why. Students who are interested in music may want to research songs of the Holocaust and musicians who lived during that time.

Additional Books: Junior High/ Middle School Level

Gavriel and Jamal. Two Boys of Jerusalem by Brent Ashabranner. Photographs by Paul Conklin. (E)

Gentlehands by M. E. Kerr. (S)

The Old Brown Suitcase: A Teenager's Story of War and Peace by Lillian Boraks-Nemetz. (S)

Skinhead by Jay Bennett. (S)

Terrible Things by Eve Bunting. (AL)

Secondary School Level

Bennett, Jay. *Skinhead.*
Fawcett Juniper, 1991. 146 pages.

All through the flight to Seattle a voice within him kept saying, "Turn back, turn back, Jonathan.

You're making a terrible mistake.
A fatal one.
When the plane lands, turn back.
Get into another one immediately.
Return to Southhampton." (p. 8)

At a Glance ▪ Jonathan Atwood receives a strange phone call requesting that he fly immediately from his home in New York to Seattle to the deathbed of a stranger. As he tries to solve the mystery of the man who summoned him, his life is endangered by neo-Nazis. Bennett's easy-reading style combined with his action-filled accounts make this book potentially appropriate for a wide range of readers from junior high/middle school students to high school students. A suspense novel, it should appeal equally to both male and female readers.

Summary ▪ Jonathan Atwood is the grandson of one of America's wealthiest and most powerful men. He lives a privileged life in New York until he receives a mysterious phone call, summoning him to travel across the country to the bedside of a man he has never met. He arrives after the man has died, making his summons even more mysterious. The man has been beaten to death. Jonathan finds out that the dead man is a college professor named Alfred Kaplan who was writing a book to expose the neo-Nazi movement in the Pacific Northwest. Jonathan, seeking answers about the mysterious Dr. Kaplan, becomes entwined with the neo-Nazis and his life is threatened in the process.

Jonathan looked away from him to the pale blue walls, a bleak feeling rising inside him, and then he slowly turned back to the Skinhead. The rows of empty wooden chairs were behind Carl. Jonathan imagined them filled with people, people with intense faces and cold eyes, eyes of black hatred, bald, shining heads.

He imagined Carl standing erect on the platform speaking to them. Shouting. "America for Americans." . . .

Carl . . . spoke again. "Listen to me. We never touched Alfred Kaplan. I swear to you on my mother's grave. We didn't like him because he was a Jew. Jews are not pure white Americans. You know that, don't you?" (pp. 95–96)

Teaching Considerations ▪ Bennett uses a distinct style of short sentences, repetition, and short chapters. Have your students look at the style and decide how it contributes to the suspense of this book. A good companion book is *The White Power Movement: America's Racist Hate Groups* by Elaine Landau. The film/video, *Obedience,* which describes the Yale University experiments on the willingness of people to follow orders even though they inflict pain on others, could be used with this book (see chapter 7).

Boraks-Nemetz, Lillian. *The Old Brown Suitcase: A Teenager's Story of War and Peace.* Ben-Simon Publications, 1994. 148 pages.

"I bought this suitcase so that you can pack your things in it. You're getting to be a big girl Slava, who knows where this suitcase might take you someday." (p. 19)

At a Glance ▪ Slava and her family have immigrated to post-World War II Canada from their native Poland. She tells her story of the difficult changes that she endures as a teenager in a new country and one who has experienced the problems of the war. Because of the age of the protagonist, secondary school students as well as junior high school/middle school students will enjoy this book.

Summary ▪ Slava tells the story of her family's immigration to Canada and their first two years there. The chapters about life after the war are juxtaposed with chapters about her experiences during the war. As she tells of the adjustments to a new country, a new language, and a new school experience, she remembers her life in Warsaw before the war, in the ghetto, in hiding, and in Warsaw after the war. Although she comes from an educated, wealthy family, they still had to struggle after the war. Slava has problems adapting to school and making new friends because she is hiding her past.

He shook his head sorrowfully. "It is hard to believe that the German people could have brought themselves to commit such crimes as they did under the Nazis. Yet they did. Sometimes people do terrible things, but we must believe that goodness in man will prevail over evil, and that your classmates can learn the difference between the two. The letter certainly proves that they can learn." (p. 84)

Teaching Considerations ▪ This book presents many of the difficulties that anyone experiences going into a new situation, but Slava's history compounds her difficulties. Have students relate their experiences of being in a new situation or dealing with a newcomer. The postwar experiences of Johanna Reiss, Ruth Sender, Ida Vos, and Aranka Siegal make good companion books (see entries in this chapter).

Kerr, M. E. *Gentlehands.*
HarperCollins, 1978; Harper Keypoint, 1990. 183 pages.

"Grandpa Trenker doesn't seem like such a snob." I'd met him only twice, once when I was little, and don't remember; once when my mother took me to see him in Montauk. He lives in this huge house by the ocean. He seems all right to me, one of these foreign types with classical music going and a lot of talk about his gardens. I couldn't wait to leave, though, because my mother was so uncomfortable around him. She just thought I ought to meet him, she said; he is your grandfather, she said, and he doesn't have two heads or anything, so you'll see for yourself. (pp. 8–9)

At a Glance ▪ Buddy Boyle makes connections with his grandfather, a cultured, wealthy European, to impress his wealthy new girlfriend. Buddy grows very fond of his grandfather and then he finds out that he has a secret, a terrible secret. This book is appropriate for high school students and some middle school students.

Summary ▪ Buddy isn't getting along with his parents. They disapprove of his new girlfriend, Skye Pennington. She is very rich and "out of their class." They are afraid that Buddy will start putting on airs like his grandfather. In an effort to impress his wealthy, sophisticated girlfriend, Buddy decides to take her to visit his grandfather. Although he has only seen him twice, Buddy remembers that his grandfather is a cultured, urbane European. He knows that will impress Skye. Buddy discovers that he likes his grandfather and finds him to be a fountain of knowledge, a person who can teach him many things. His parents object to his relationships with his grandfather and with Skye. Buddy resents their attitude and decides to move in with his grandfather, who has a gentleness and gift with birds and wild animals. Buddy and his grandfather get to be good friends during the time he stays with him, but the grandfather has a secret. He was a Nazi official, ironically called "Gentlehands" by his victims at Auschwitz because of how he toyed with their emotions just before he had them executed. A Nazi hunter is looking for Gentlehands and his identity is revealed. Buddy must make sense of the revelations about the past and the man he knows.

> My grandfather did everything well, including cook. He served us a filet of fish in spinach with shrimp and mushrooms, and a salad of fresh bean sprouts from his garden. In the center of the table he put a bouquet of red and pink roses he'd cut from the vines outside the patio. We all had a glass of wine with the meal, and instead of opera playing on the tape he had Strauss waltzes. (p. 106)

Teaching Considerations ▪ The book demonstrates a discrepancy between appearance and reality. Help your students to examine the characters in this novel within the context of that discrepancy. Then help them to relate their insights to contemporary situations. Also have your students discuss the significance of making the grandfather a Nazi war criminal rather that some other type of criminal.

Voigt, Cynthia. *David and Jonathan.*
Scholastic, 1992. 249 pages.

> "A boy then, fourteen he weighed sixty-six pounds. He'd been living in the displaced persons camp. He was—the doctors said he would need special care, special treatments— he didn't want to eat, he couldn't sleep. Nobody knew how to help him . . . .We knew what had happened to all the others," Mrs. Nafiche said. Her eyes wept. "He was the only one we'd been unable to learn anything of. So there was hope." (pp. 53–54)

At a Glance ▪ Henry is from an old New England family, but his best friend Jonathan is a Jew. Their close friendship is disrupted when Jonathan's cousin David, the only member of his mother's family to survive the Holocaust, comes to live with them. This book is appropriate for high school students; however, the relationships between David and both Henry and Jonathan are difficult and might be perplexing and confusing to them. This novel is a complex interweaving of a number of themes and strands.

Summary ▪ The book is set in the 1950s. Two high school students are close friends, in spite of the differences in their backgrounds. Jonathan is a Jew whose mother had to escape from Nazi Germany while his best friend, Henry, is from an old, established New England family. Jonathan's family provides a home for his cousin, David, a Holocaust survivor. David is a haunted and disturbed young man who challenges both Henry and Jonathan to reexamine their lives.

> Jon added quietly, "Hank. We've served, and we survived. We've survived David—I have and I think you can—and we've survived this war—which is our war, whatever we may think of it. And I don't think much of it, truth be told. We should be drinking wine, out among the dancing women. The glass is half full." (p. 244)

Teaching Considerations ▪ It is difficult often for youthful readers to imagine the ongoing grief and pain that the Holocaust caused. To help your students recognize the problems that the Holocaust continued to cause Jonathan's family, have them find specific quotes from the book that express what the family feels. The film/ video, *About the Holocaust,* narrated by the American daughter of a survivor, can be used effectively with this book.

Additional Books: Secondary School Level

Chernowitz! by Fran Arrick. (JM)

Grace in the Wilderness: After the Liberation 1945–48 by Aranka Siegal. (JM)

The Mozart Season by Virginia Euwer Wolff. (JM)

Terrible Things by Eve Bunting. (AL)

To Life by Ruth Minsky Sender. (JM)

Tunes for Bears to Dance to by Robert Cormier. (JM)

Further Reading for All Levels

Bush, Lawrence. *Rooftop Secrets and Other Stories of Anti-Semitism*. Union of American Hebrew Congregations, 1986. 157 pages. (E, JM)

This collection of eight stories traces the history of the persecution of Jews from the time of Columbus in the fifteenth century to contemporary times. The eight short stories are appropriate for elementary school children or junior high/middle school students because they are written from the perspective of a Jewish child facing prejudice. Each story is introduced with an historical overview and followed by a thorough discussion of the lesson to be learned. The discussion is frequently didactic and teachers should be aware of this potential problem. They should closely supervise student reading of these stories.

CityKids Foundation. *CityKids Speak on Prejudice*. Random House, 1994. 44 pages. (JM, S)

In the words of urban high school students, mostly from New York City, issues of prejudice, stereotyping, self-identity, gender, faith, and pride are presented in this book. Factual data on prejudice is juxtaposed with the reactions of young people in personal narratives, poetry, and responses.

Hesse, Karen. *Letters from Rifka*. Henry Holt, 1992; Puffin Books, 1993. 148 pages. (E, JM)

Winner of numerous awards, this book is based on the memories of the author's great-aunt whose family had to flee Russia due to the cruel treatment of Jews. When Rifka and her family secretly leave their village in Russia in September, 1919, Rifka, then twelve, writes about their dangerous escape in letters to her cousin Tovah. Even though she knows she cannot send the letters, writing helps her feel less lonely and frightened. The family faces many dangers and hardships as it journeys to America, not the least of which is having to leave Rifka in Belgium for many months until the doctor certifies that her ringworm is cured and she can travel. But when Rifka finally arrives on Ellis Island, the doctors there detain her again because her hair has not grown back. They fear she may not be able to attract a husband to support her and thus will become a burden on the government.

Hillel, Shlomo. *Operation Babylon.* Translated from the Hebrew by Ina Friedman. Doubleday, 1987. 301 pages. (S)

This nonfiction account details the rescue of Iraqi Jews. From 1947 to 1952, 95 percent of the Jewish community of Iraq immigrated to Israel. Their journey was complicated by politics. In the early days, before the establishment of the Jewish state, they had to be smuggled out of Iraq and then smuggled past the British ban on immigrants to Palestine. The overland routes were then closed, even after the establishment of Israel, so from 1948 to 1950 emigrants from Iraq had to be airlifted. From 1950 to 1952 the political situation eased and most of the remaining members of the Iraqi Jewish community emigrated.

Lakin, Patricia. Illustrated by Ted Rand. *Don't Forget.* Tambourine Books, 1994. 27 pages. (P)

In this picture book, Sarah visits local shops in her multicultural neighborhood, buying the ingredients for her first cake, a surprise for her mother's birthday. Among the shops is the grocery store of Mr. and Mrs. Singer who have blue numbers tattooed on their arms. The Singers help Sarah to realize that as painful as the past is, it must never be forgotten.

Lasky, Kathryn. Illustrated by Trina Schart Hyman. *The Night Journey.* Frederick Warne, 1981; Puffin Books, 1986. 150 pages. (JM, E)

In a story set in contemporary times, Rachel, thirteen, finds the time she must spend with her great-grandmother, Nana Sashie, boring. Then Nana begins to tell her stories of her childhood in Russia. Rachel's parents don't want Nana Sashie talking about the past, but Rachel is intrigued when she discovers that her great-great-great-grandparents were murdered by soldiers because they were Jews. Rachel spends more and more time with Nana as she learns how in 1900 nine-year-old Sashie devised an escape plan for her family. Winner of several awards, this book helps young people understand the value of learning about their past.

Landau, Elaine. *The White Power Movement: America's Racist Hate Groups.* Millbrook Press, 1993. 96 pages. (S)

This nonfiction account of hate groups includes an explanation of the roots of racism and its causes in this country. In addition, it documents the rise of hate crimes in this decade. It has a useful bibliography and lists the names and addresses of groups combating racism.

Levitin, Sonia. *The Return*. Fawcett Juniper Books, 1987. 181 pages. (JM, S)

As Ethiopian Jews, Desta and her family are called strangers in their native land and they live in poverty and persecution in a remote mountain village. The drought has made life hard throughout the country and conditions under the Communists have become even more difficult for them. Visitors come to their village and talk about the Promised Land of Jerusalem where they can be free to worship and to live as they wish. Desta's older brother, Joas, is determined to escape although it means walking for weeks through the mountains and jungles to get to the border of Sudan where they will wait to be transported to Israel. Joas, Desta, and their younger sister prepare for the long, dangerous journey, seeking the company and protection of friends from a neighboring community, but much of their trip is alone. This story of courage and faith demonstrates that persecution continues even today.

Levoy, Myron. *Alan and Naomi*. Harper & Row, 1977. 192 pages. (JM, E)

Set in New York City in 1944, this is the story of Alan Silverman, a bright, studious boy who is mainly concerned with playing stickball with the other junior high boys and with not being called a sissy. His life gets complicated when his parents ask him to spend time with Naomi Kirshenbaum, a young French refugee whose horrifying experiences, including witnessing the murder of her father by the Nazis, have left her deeply disturbed. To see any girl, let alone a crazy-acting one like Naomi, will make Alan vulnerable to teasing and ridicule by the other boys. Alan does spend time with Naomi, initially keeping it a secret, and eventually is able to gain her trust and help her begin to recover. But when she and Alan are attacked on their way to school, she is terrified and disappears. Alan learns many important lessons about courage and what is important in this touching story. See entry for the film/video version in chapter 7 of this book.

Loumaye, Jacqueline. *Chagall: My Sad and Joyous Village*. Translated by John Goodman. Chelsea House, 1994. 63 pages. (E, JM)

Nicholas shares stories of his home in Russia with his young friend, Giles. He shows him prints of the work of his fellow Russian, artist Marc Chagall. He also tells Giles the story of Chagall's life, beginning with his childhood in Russia when he discovered that he wanted to be a painter. He traces Chagall's life as a student with Bakst in Saint Petersburg to his years in Paris where he went to paint. Then he tells of Chagall's stay in New York City during World War II, where he fled to avoid the horrors of the Nazis. Nicholas also relates the latter years of the painter's life. The book has three types of illustrations: first, prints of Chagall's work; second, a few photographs from his life; and third, the illustrations of Nicholas with Giles as he relates Chagall's story.

Provost, Gary, and Gail Levine-Provost. *David and Max.* Jewish Publication Society, 1988. 180 pages. (JM, E)

In this contemporary story, David has a close and loving relationship with his grandfather, Max Levene, a wonderfully witty and colorful man. The family has never talked much about Max's life in Europe during World War II, until the summer Max thinks he sees an old friend whom he believed had died in the Holocaust over forty years ago. Gradually, Max tells David about this terrible time and helps him to understand the decisions people had to make. In the process, David learns about himself and what is important in life. Told from David's perspective, this is a tremendously appealing story that helps today's youth understand events that happened long before they were born, but still have consequences for them today. *Good If It Goes,* by the same authors, can be used in conjunction with *David and Max.* Winner of the 1984 National Jewish Book Award, it describes David's preparation for his bar mitzvah as he learns about his heritage and what is important to him.

Reiss, Johanna. *The Journey Back.* HarperCollins, 1976. 212 pages. (JM, S)

In this novel, the sequel to *The Upstairs Room,* Annie quickly realizes that while the war may be over, its impact continues. After three years in hiding, the adjustment to life is difficult. Her mother has died and before long her father remarries. Annie does not get along with her new stepmother. Her sisters are changing and they must make a life in a new home.

Sender, Ruth Minsky. *The Holocaust Lady.* Macmillan, 1992.
192 pages. (JM)

This novel joins the two previously published Sender books, *The Cage* and *To Life,* both personal narratives of her own experiences during the Holocaust. In this book the main character is an English teacher, the only surviving member of her family who were incarcerated in a concentration camp during World War II. She is compelled to tell her story to her students, demonstrating the need to bear witness to the horrors.

Stern, Guy. *Nazi Book Burning and the American Response.*
Wayne State University, 1989. 17 pages. (S)

In this Distinguished Lecture, Professor Stern at Wayne State University examines both the immediate and long-term American reactions to the Nazis' book burnings throughout Germany on May 10, 1933. Initial responses failed to recognize that these burnings were the product of a regime for whom violence and especially fire would be much-used weapons. This speech would be appropriate for secondary school students to analyze in recognizing the impact of this act and its symbolism.

Strasser, Todd. *The Wave.* Laurel-Leaf Library, 1981. 143 pages (S)

This novelization of a television drama is based on an actual classroom situation that occurred in 1969 during a unit on World War II in a high school history class. The teacher creates a simulation to demonstrate to his students how Nazism gained influence in Germany. This simulation or experiment, called the Wave, is the basis for this fictionalized account in which the teacher uses it to propose a new system of rigid rules and regulations. Students have a special salute, a code of behavior, and a slogan that defines their philosophy: "Strength through Discipline, Strength through Community." By establishing a sense of community in the classroom, students gain a sense of belonging and soon the Wave is attracting other students. The experiment gains a life of its own, and the teacher realizes that action needs to be taken to stop it. See entry on the film/video in chapter 7.

Vos, Ida. *Anna Is Still Here.* Translated by Terese Edelstein and Inez Smidt. Houghton Mifflin, 1986, 1993. 139 pages. (JM)

In this sequel to *Hide and Seek*, Ida Vos explores what it is like to be a survivor of the Holocaust. Anna was in hiding for several years while the Nazis occupied Holland. Now the war is over, but Anna, age thirteen, is having difficulty adjusting. She makes friends with a lonely woman and together they learn to move beyond their pasts.

Yolen, Jane. *Briar Rose*. Tom Doherty Associates, 1992. 200 pages (S, JM)

Winner of several awards, *Briar Rose* is a contemporary novel that links the German fairy tale of Briar Rose (or Sleeping Beauty) with the Holocaust. Throughout their childhood, Gemma (Grandma) told her three granddaughters the story of Briar Rose. With her death, Becca, the youngest and a reporter, is determined to discover the truth of her grandmother's stories and her heritage, of which even her mother is uncertain. Gemma had always refused to talk about her life before coming to America, and at her death left only a few clues in a wooden box with a carving of briar and a rose on the cover. Becca's quest leads her to old friends of her grandmother and finally to Poland, where she learns of her grandmother's remarkable survival.

Literature Involvement:
Suggestions and Issues for Responding
and Thinking

The books included in this chapter present a sampling of fiction and nonfiction that demonstrates the ongoing impact of the Holocaust and other acts of discrimination. Young people need opportunities to reflect upon what they are learning and to express their feelings. They also need opportunities to clarify misconceptions and to seek additional information. The following suggestions can be selected according to their appropriateness for the various age groups and then used to provide these opportunities:

- One of the justifications that we heard from the members of the Third Reich was: "I was just following orders." Is this a valid excuse for the Holocaust? When is it morally right to abandon one's own beliefs and values to obey an external order?

- Certainly followers of Hitler would believe the old cliche "the ends justify the means." What were the ends that he sought, and how might you prove that the means were wrong?

- Collect information about hate crimes from the newspapers or news accounts on television. What do these crimes have in common? What similarities are there among the groups (or individuals) who commit them?

- Virtually everyone has encountered a bully at one time or another. Recount any experience you've had or observed. How did it make you feel? What action did you want to take? What action did you take?

- While the Nazis fell short of their goal to destroy all European Jews, they did have a devastating impact. Identify the setting from one of the books you have read. Research what happened to the Jewish population in that area.

- What is meant by "For many survivors, liberation wasn't the end of their suffering, but a beginning of a different kind of suffering?"

- Why did the establishment of the state of Israel become such a significant issue after the war?

- Read accounts of relocations of survivors. What kinds of experiences did they have?

- Select a quotation from one of the books you read. What does it mean? What is its significance for you? (In a classroom setting, students can write their selections on the chalkboard or on paper strips to display on the walls. These can then be used to prompt group discussion and as a springboard for writing.)

7

We Learn from Other Sources

Organizations and Institutions; Curriculum Guides, Journals, and Other Educational Materials; Media Resources—Films/Videos, Audio Recordings

> But the Holocaust is a fact of modern history, and now all
> of us . . . must face that fact. It could happen anywhere,
> even in nations that think of themselves as highly "civilized."
> Learning about it can help to prevent it.
>
> Seymour Rossel, *The Holocaust: The Fire That Raged*

There are many ways to help young people learn about the Holocaust. While the literature of the Holocaust is the primary focus of this book, this chapter provides information about other resources that can be used effectively in conjunction with the literature described in the preceding chapters. Indeed, we believe that learning is most effective when young people are given multiple opportunities and a variety of approaches to a topic. This chapter is organized into four major categories: organizations and institutions; curriculum guides, journals, and other educational materials; other sources; and media resources, consisting of films/videos and audio recordings.

Organizations and Institutions

The organizations and institutions listed below are useful places to contact for information. They provide a variety of services, including in some cases, specific teaching materials and training sessions.

Aaron H. Leibtag Resource
Center
Board of Jewish Education
Building
5800 Park Heights
Baltimore, MD 21209

Allentown Jewish Archives
Holocaust Resource Center
702 N. 22nd Street
Allentown, PA 18014
Tel 215-821-5500
Fax 215-821-8946

American Friends of the Ghetto
Fighters' House
P.O. Box 2153
765 Queen Anne Road
Teaneck, NJ 07666
Tel 201-836-1910
Fax 201-801-0786

American Gathering of Jewish
Holocaust Survivors
122 W. 30th Street,
Suite 205
New York, NY 10001
Tel 212-239-4230
Fax 212-279-2926

American Jewish Archives
3101 Clifton Avenue
Cincinnati, OH 45215
Tel 513-221-1875

American Red Cross
Holocaust and War Victims
Tracing and Information Center
American Red Cross
Central Maryland Chapter
4700 Mount Hope Drive
Baltimore, MD 21215
Tel 301-764-5311
800-848-9277
Fax 410-764-4638

American Society for Yad
Vashem
48 West 37th Street,
9th Floor
New York, NY 10018
Tel 212-564-9606
Fax 212-564-6395

Anne Frank Center, USA
584 Broadway, Suite 408
New York, NY 10012
Tel 212-431-8249
Fax 212-431-8375
E-mail 72550.3225@
compuserv.com

Anne Frank Institute of
Philadelphia
401 N. Broad Street,
5th Floor
Philadelphia, PA 19108
Tel 215-238-5379
Fax 215-238-5340

The Annual Scholar's
Conference on the Holocaust
and the Churches
P.O. Box 2147
Philadelphia, PA 19103
Tel 610-667-5437
Fax 610-667-0265

Anti-Defamation League of
B'nai B'rith
International Center for
Holocaust Studies
823 United Nations Plaza
New York, NY 10017
Tel 212-490-2525
Fax 212-867-0779

Association of Holocaust
Organizations
Holocaust Resource Center
and Archives
Queensborough Community
College
Bayside, NY 11364-1497
Tel 718-225-0378
Fax 718-631-6306

Auschwitz Study Foundation,
Inc.
P.O. Box 2232
Huntington Beach,
CA 92647
Tel 714-848-1101
Fax 714-842-1979

Baltimore Jewish Council
5750 Park Heights Avenue
Baltimore, MD 21215
Tel 410-542-4850
Fax 410-542-4834

Center for Holocaust and
Genocide Studies
Ramapo College Library
505 Ramapo Valley Road
Mahwah, NJ 07430
Tel 201-529-7409
Fax 201-529-6717

Center for Holocaust Studies
Brookdale Community
College
765 Newman Spring Road
Lincroft, NJ 07738
Tel 908-224-2769

Commission on Holocaust
Remembrance of Agudath Israel
of America
84 William Street
New York, NY
Tel 212-797-9000, ext. 31
Fax 212-269-2843

Fred R. Crawford
Witness to the Holocaust
Project
Emory University
Atlanta, GA 30322
Tel 404-329-6428

The Dallas Memorial Center
for Holocaust Studies
7900 Northaven Road
Dallas, TX 75230
Tel 214-750-4654
Fax 214-750-4672

Dayton Holocaust Resource
Center
100 East Woodbury Drive
Dayton, OH 45415
Tel 513-278-7444
Fax 513-832-2121

Drew University Center for
Holocaust Study
Rose Memorial Library
Madison, NJ 07940
Tel 201-408-3600
Fax 201-408-3768

El Paso Holocaust Museum
and Study Center
  405 Wallenberg Drive
  El Paso, TX 79912
  Tel 915-833-5656
  Fax 915-584-0243

Facing History and Ourselves
National Foundation Inc.
  16 Hurd Road
  Brookline, MA 02146
  Tel 617-232-1595
  Fax 617-232-0281

Fortunoff Video Archive for
Holocaust Testimonies
  Sterling Memorial Library
  Yale University
  P.O. Box 802840
  New Haven, CT 06520-
  8240
  Tel 203-432-1879
  E-mail joanner@yalevm.ycc.
  yale.edu

Friends of Le Chambon
  8033 Sunset Boulevard
  Suite 784
  Los Angeles, CA 90046
  Tel 213-650-1774
  Fax 213-654-4689

Georgia Commission on the
Holocaust
  2520 E. Piedmont Road,
  Suite F-179
  Marietta, GA 30062
  Tel 404-651-9273
  Fax 404-657-8427

Greater Cincinnati Interfaith
Holocaust Foundation
  3101 Clifton Avenue
  Cincinnati, OH 45220
  Tel 513-221-1875
  Fax 513-221-7812

Halina Wind Preston Holocaust
Education Center
  101 Garden of Eden Road
  Wilmington, DE 19803
  Tel 302-478-6200
  Fax 302-478-5374

The Hawaii Holocaust Project
  W.S. Richardson
  School of Law
  University of Hawaii,
  Manoa
  2515 Dole Street
  Honolulu, HI 96822
  Tel 808-956-6994
  Fax 808-956-6402

Hidden Child Foundation/ADL
  823 United Nations Plaza
  New York, NY 10017
  Tel 212-490-2525
  Fax 212-867-0779

Holocaust Archives California
State University Library
  California State University
  Fullerton, CA 92631

Holocaust Awareness Institute
  University of Denver
  Denver, CO 80208
  Tel 303-871-3013
  Fax 303-871-3037

Learning About the Holocaust

Holocaust Awareness Museum
    Gratz College
    Old York Road and
    Melrose Avenue
    Melrose Park, PA 19027
    Tel 215-635-6480
    Fax 215-635-7320

Holocaust Center of the North
Shore Jewish Federation
    McCarthy School
    70 Lake Street, Room 108
    Peabody, MA 01960
    Tel 508-535-0003

Holocaust Center of Northern
California
    639 14th Avenue
    San Francisco, CA 94118
    Tel 415-751-6040
    Fax 415-751-6983

Holocaust Center of the
United Jewish Federation
of Greater Pittsburgh
    242 McKee Place
    Pittsburgh, PA 15213
    Tel 412-682-7111
    Fax 412-681-3980

Holocaust, Child Survivors of
Connecticut, Inc.
    Marcelle Bock
    235 Chestnut Hill Road
    Wilton, CT 06897
    Tel 203-762-8734

Holocaust Documentation
and Education Center, Inc.
    Florida International
    University
    North Miami Campus
    3000 N.E. 145 Street
    North Miami, FL 33181
    Tel 305-940-5690
    Fax 305-940-5691

Holocaust Education Center
    State Teachers College
    Seminar Hakibbutzim
    Namir Road 149
    Tel Aviv, Israel 62057
    Tel 972-3-6902369
    Fax 972-3-6990269

Holocaust Education and
Memorial Centre of Toronto
    4600 Bathurst Street
    Willowdale, Ontario M2R
    3V2
    Canada
    Tel 416-635-2883
    Fax 416-635-1408

Holocaust Education Center
and Memorial Museum of
Houston
    2425 Fountainview Drive,
    Suite 270
    Houston, TX 77057-4811
    Tel 713-789-9898
    Fax 713-789-8502

Holocaust Education
Foundation
    3130 Big Tree Lane
    Wilmette, IL 60091
    Tel 708-251-1952

Holocaust Education Resource
Center
    College of Saint Elizabeth
    2 Convent Road
    Morristown, NJ 07960
    Tel 201-292-6390
    Fax 201-292-6777
    E-mail Sepinwall@
    liza.st-elizabeth.edu

Holocaust/Genocide Studies
Center
    Plainview/Old Bethpage
    John F. Kennedy
    High School
    50 Kennedy Drive
    Plainview, NY 11803
    Tel 516-937-6382

Holocaust-Genocide Studies
Project
    Monroe Community
    College
    1000 East Henrietta Road
    Rochester, NY 14623
    Tel 716-292-3228
    Fax 716-427-2749

Holocaust Human Rights
Center of Maine
    RR 1, Box 825
    Palermo, ME 04354
    Tel 207-993-2620

Holocaust Learning Center
    David Posnack
    Jewish Center
    5850 South Pine
    Island Road
    Davie, FL 33328
    Tel 305-434-0499
    Fax 305-434-1741

Holocaust Library and
Research Center
    601 14th Avenue
    San Francisco, CA 94103

Holocaust Memorial Center
Detroit Jewish Community
Center
    6600 W. Maple Road
    West Bloomfield, MI 48322
    Tel 313-661-0840
    Fax 313-661-4202

Holocaust Memorial Center
Florida International University
    Bay Vista Campus
    NE 155 Street and
    Biscayne Boulevard
    Miami, FL 33181

Holocaust Memorial
Committee of Brooklyn
    4089 Ocean Avenue
    Brooklyn, NY 11235
    Tel 718-934-4790

Holocaust Memorial and
Educational Center
of Nassau County
    Welwyn Preserve
    100 Crescent Beach Road
    Glen Cove, NY 11542
    Tel 516-571-8040
    Fax 516-571-8041

Holocaust Memorial
Foundation of Illinois
    4255 West Main Street
    Skokie, IL 60076-2063
    Tel 708-677-4640
    Fax 708-677-4684

Holocaust Memorial Resource
and Education Center of
Central Florida
  851 N. Maitland Avenue
  Maitland, FL 32751
  Tel 407-628-0555

Holocaust Museum and
Learning Center of St. Louis
  12 Millstone Campus Drive
  St. Louis, MO 63146
  Tel 314-432-0020
  Fax 314-432-1244

Holocaust Oral History Archive
of Gratz College
  Old York Road and
  Melrose Avenue
  Melrose Park, PA 19027
  Tel 215-635-7300
  Fax 215-635-7320

Holocaust Oral History Project
  P.O. Box 77603
  San Francisco, CA 94107
  Tel 415-882-7092

Holocaust Oral History Project
University of Michigan at
Dearborn
  Marigian Library
  Dearborn, MI 48128
  Tel 313-593-5000

Holocaust Resource Center
  Bureau of Jewish Education
  441 East Avenue
  Rochester, NY 14607
  Tel 716-461-0290
  Fax 716-461-0912

Holocaust Resource Center and
Archives
  Queensborough Community
  College
  222-05 56th Avenue
  Bayside, NY 11364
  Tel 718-225-1617
  Fax 718-631-6306

Holocaust Resource Center of
Buffalo
  2640 North Forest Road
  Getzville, NY 14068
  Tel 716-688-7020
  Fax 716-634-0592

Holocaust Resource Center of
Greater Toledo
  6465 Sylvania Avenue
  P.O. Box 587
  Sylvania, OH 43560
  Tel 419-885-4485
  Fax 419-885-3207

Holocaust Resource Center of
the JCRC of South Jersey
  2393 W. Marlton Pike
  Cherry Hill, NJ 08002
  Tel 609-665-6100
  Fax 609-665-0074

Holocaust Resource Center of
the Jewish Federation of
Greater Clifton-Passaic
  199 Scoles Avenue
  Clifton, NJ 07012
  Tel 201-777-7031
  Fax 201-777-6701

Holocaust Resource Center of
Kean College
    Thompson Library
    Kean College
    Union, NJ 07083
    Tel 908-527-3049

Holocaust Resource Center of
Keen State College
    Mason Library
    Keene State College
    Box 3201, 229 Main Street
    Keene, NH 03435-3201
    Tel 603-358-2490
    Fax 603-358-2743

Holocaust Resource Center of
Minneapolis
    8200 West 33rd Street
    Minneapolis, MN 55426
    Tel 612-935-0316
    Fax 612-935-0319

Holocaust Resource Center
The Richard Stockton College
of New Jersey
    Pomona, NJ 08240
    Tel 609-652-4699
    Fax 609-652-4958

Holocaust Studies Center
    The Bronx High School
    of Science
    75 West 205th Street
    Bronx, NY 10468
    Tel 212-367-5252

Holocaust Survivors and
Friends in Pursuit of Justice, Inc.
    800 New Loudon Road,
    Suite #400
    Latham, NY 12110
    Tel 518-785-0035

Interfaith Council on
the Holocaust
    125 South 9th Street,
    Suite 300
    Philadelphia, PA 19107
    Tel 215-922-7222
    Fax 215-440-7680

International Alert Against
Genocide
    1015 Gayley Avenue
    Box 259
    Los Angeles, CA 90024

International Network of
Children of Jewish Holocaust
Survivors, Inc.
    Florida International
    University
    North Miami Campus—
    SC 130
    N.E. 151st Street and
    Biscayne Boulevard
    North Miami, FL 33181
    Tel 305-940-5690
    Fax 305-940-5691

International Study for
Organized Persecution
of Children
    30 Soundview Drive
    Sands Point, NY 11050
    Tel 516-883-7135
    Fax 516-883-3850

Jewish Federation of Greater
New Haven
    360 Amity Road
    Woodbridge, CT
    06525-2136
    Tel 203-387-2424
    Fax 203-387-1818

Jewish Federation of
Las Vegas Holocaust
Education Committee
   3909 S. Maryland Parkway
   Suite 400
   Las Vegas, NV 89119-7520
   Tel 702-732-0556
   Fax 702-732-3228

Jewish Foundation for Christian
Rescuers, ADL
   823 United Nations Plaza
   New York, NY 10017
   Tel 212-490-2525
   Fax 212-867-0779

Jewish Labor Committee
   25 East 21st Street
   New York, NY 10010
   Tel 212-477-0707
   Fax 212-477-1918

Joseph H. and Belle R. Braun
Center of Holocaust Studies
   Anti-Defamation League of
   B'nai B'rith
   823 United Nations Plaza
   New York, NY 10017
   Tel 212-490-2525
   Fax 212-867-0779

The Julius and Dorothy
Koppelman Holocaust/
Genocide Resource Center
   Rider College
   2083 Lawrenceville Road
   Lawrenceville, NJ 08648
   Tel 609-896-5345
   Fax 609-895-5684

Kent State University,
Main Library
   Audio Visual Service
   Kent, OH 44242
   Tel 216-672-3456

Laszio Tauber Institute
   Brandeis University
   Waltham, MA 02254

Leo Baeck Institute
   129 East 73rd Street
   New York, NY 10021
   Tel 212-744-6400
   Fax 212-988-1305

A Living Memorial to the
Holocaust Museum of Jewish
Heritage
   342 Madison Avenue,
   Suite 706
   New York, NY 10173
   Tel 212-687-9141
   Fax 212-573-9847

Martyrs Memorial and
Museum of the Holocaust
of the Jewish Federation
Council
   Jewish Community Building
   6505 Wilshire Boulevard
   Los Angeles, CA 90048
   Tel 213-852-3242
   Fax 213-951-0349

Metrowest Holocaust
Education and Remembrance
Council
   901 Route 10
   Whippany, NJ 07981
   Tel 201-884-4800
   Fax 201-884-7361

Joseph Meyerhoff Library
Baltimore Hebrew University
   5800 Park Heights Avenue
   Baltimore, MD 21215
   Tel 301-578-6936
   Fax 301-578-6940

Midwest Center for Holocaust
Education
    5801 W. 115 Street,
    Suite 106
    Overland Park, KS 66211
    Tel 913-491-9665
    Fax 913-491-9742

Montreal Holocaust
Memorial Centre
    Allied Jewish Community
    Services'
    Cummings House
    5151 Côte Sainte
    Catherine Road
    Montreal, Quebec H3W
    1M6
    Canada
    Tel 514-345-2605
    Fax 514-344-2651

National Association for
Holocaust Education
    West Chester University
    West Chester, PA 19383
    Tel 215-436-2789

The National Catholic Center
for Holocaust Education
    Seton Hill College
    Greensburg, PA 15601
    Tel 412-830-1033
    Fax 412-838-4611

Netherlands State Institute
for War Documentation
    POB 19769, 1000 GT
    Amsterdam, Netherlands

Nevada Governor's Advisory
Council on Education Relating
to the Holocaust
    3909 S. Maryland Parkway,
    Suite 400
    Las Vegas, NV 89118-7520
    Tel 702-732-0556
    Fax 702-732-3228

New England Holocaust
Memorial Committee
    59 Temple Place, Suite 608
    Boston, MA 02111
    Tel 617-338-2288
    Fax 617-338-6885

North Carolina Council on the
Holocaust
    Department of Human
    Resources
    101 Blair Drive
    Raleigh, NC 27603
    Tel 919-733-2173
    Fax 919-733-7447

Oregon Holocaust Resource
Center
    2900 SW Peaceful Lane
    Portland, OR 97201
    Tel 503-244-6284
    Fax 503-246-7553

The Philadephia Center on the
Holocaust Genocide and
Human Rights
    P.O. Box 2147
    Philadelphia, PA 19103
    Tel 215-667-5437
    Fax 215-667-0265

Ratner Media Center
    2030 South Taylor Road
    Cleveland Heights,
    OH 44118
    Tel 216-371-8288

Learning About the Holocaust

Rhode Island Holocaust
Memorial Museum
JCC of Rhode Island
401 Elmgrove Avenue
Providence, RI 02906
Tel 401-861-8800
Fax 401-331-7961

Rockland Center for Holocaust
Studies, Inc.
17 South Madison Avenue
Spring Valley, NY 10977
Tel 914-356-2700
Fax 914-356-1974

The Rosen Holocaust Center of
Southern California
1385 Warner Avenue,
Suite A
Tustin, CA 92680-6442
Tel 714-259-0655
Fax 714-259-1635

The Rosenthal Institute for
Holocaust Studies
Graduate School and
University Center, CUNY
33 West 42nd Street, Room
1516GB
New York, NY 10036
Tel 212-642-2183

St. Louis Center for Holocaust
Studies
12 Millstone Campus Drive
St. Louis, MO 63146
Tel 314-431-0020
Fax 314-432-1277

Seidman Educational Resource
Center of the Auerbach Central
Agency for Jewish Education
7607 Old York Road
Melrose Park, PA 19027
Tel 215-635-8940
Fax 215-635-8946

Simon Wiesenthal Center for
Holocaust Studies
Yeshiva University
9760 West Pico Boulevard
Los Angeles, CA 90035
Tel 310-553-9036
Fax 310-533-8007
E-mail simonwie@class.org

Sonoma State University
Holocaust Studies Center
1801 East Cotati Avenue
Rohnert Park, CA 94928
Tel 707-664-4076
Fax 707-664-2505

South Carolina Council on the
Holocaust
P.O. Box 50,008
Columbia, SC 29201
Tel 803-252-2782
Fax 803-252-5320

Swedish Association of
Holocaust Survivors
P.O. Box 34036
100 26 Stockholm
Sweden

Tampa Bay Holocaust
Memorial Museum
and Educational Center
5001-113th Street
Madeira Beach, FL 33708
Tel 813-392-4678
Fax 813-393-0236

Temple Judea of Manhasset
Holocaust Resource Center
333 Searington Road
Manhasset, NY 11030
Tel 516-621-8048

Tennessee Holocaust
Commission
　P.O. Box 6311, Station B
　Nashville, TN 37235
　Tel 615-343-2563
　Fax 615-343-8355

Tribute to the Danes and
Other Rescuers
　1185 Park Avenue
　New York, NY 10028
　Tel 212-348-7720
　Fax 212-348-2973

United States Holocaust
Memorial Museum
　100 Raoul Wallenberg
　Place, SW
　Washington, DC 20024-
　2150
　Tel 202-488-0400
　Fax 202-488-2690

Vancouver Holocaust Centre
for Education and
Remembrance
　950 West 41st Avenue
　Vancouver, BC V5Z 2N7
　Canada
　Tel 604-264-0499
　Fax 604-264-0487

The Vanderbilt University
Holocaust Art Collection
　Vanderbilt University
　402 Sarratt Student Center
　Nashville, TN 37240
　Tel 615-322-2471
　Fax 615-343-8081

Washington State Holocaust
Education Resource Center
　2031 Third Avenue
　Seattle, WA 98121
　Tel 206-441-5747
　Fax 206-443-0303

Westchester Holocaust
Commission
　c/o Westchester County
　Office of Cultural Affairs
　148 Martine Avenue
　White Plains, NY 10601
　Tel 914-285-3383
　Fax 914-285-2939

The West Volusia Holocaust
Memorial Council, Inc.
　P.O. Box 4045
　De Land, FL 32723
　Tel 904-734-1926

Yad Vashem, The Holocaust
Martyrs' and Heroes
Remembrance Authority
　P.O. Box 3477
　Jerusalem, Israel 91034
　Tel 972-2-751611
　Fax 972-2-433511

Zachor Holocaust Center
　1753 Peachtree Road NE
　Atlanta, GA 30309
　Tel 404-873-1661
　Fax 404-874-7043

Zell Holocaust Memorial
Zell Center for Holocaust
Studies of Spertus Institute of
Jewish Studies
　618 S. Michigan Avenue
　Chicago, IL 60605
　Tel 312-922-9012
　Fax 312-922-6406

Curriculum Guides, Journals, and Other Educational Materials

Classroom Strategies for Teaching About the Holocaust

Author: Ira Zornberg
Curriculum for junior high/middle school and secondary school.

Anti-Defamation League of B'nai B'rith
ADL Materials Library
22-D Hollywood Avenue
Ho-Ho-Kus, NJ 07423
Tel 800-343-5540

DIMENSIONS: A Journal of Holocaust Studies

Articles and book reviews; teaching aid for elementary through secondary school level.

Anti-Defamation League of B'nai B'rith
ADL Materials Library
22-D Hollywood Avenue
Ho-Ho-Kus, NJ 07423
Tel 800-343-5540

End of Innocence: Anne Frank and the Holocaust

Author: Karen Shawn
Curriculum guide for junior high/middle school and secondary school.

Anti-Defamation League of B'nai B'rith
ADL Materials Library
22-D Hollywood Avenue
Ho-Ho-Kus, NJ 07423
Tel 800-343-5540

Facing History and Ourselves: Holocaust and Human Behavior

Authors: Margot Stern Strom and William S. Parsons

Facing History is a member organization of the U.S. Department of Education's National Diffusion Network; for information on institutes and workshops, contact:

Facing History and Ourselves National Foundation, Inc.
16 Hurd Road
Brookline, MA 02146
Tel 617-232-1595
Fax 617-232-0281

Holocaust and Genocide Studies

Journal published three times a year by Oxford University Press in association with U.S. Holocaust Memorial Museum.

Oxford University Press
2001 Evans Road
Cary, NC 27513
Tel 800-852-7323
Fax 919-677-1714

The Holocaust: A Guide for Pennsylvania Teachers

Pennsylvania Department of Education
333 Market Street
Harrisburg, PA 17126-0333

The Holocaust: A Guide for Teachers of History, English, and Moral Education

Authors: David Berlin and Carole Burke

Montreal Holocaust Memorial Centre
Allied Jewish Community Services' Cummings House
5151 Côte Sainte Catherine Road
Montreal, Quebec H3W 1M6
Canada
Tel 514-345-2605
Fax 514-344-2651

The Holocaust: A North Carolina Teacher's Resource

North Carolina Council on the Holocaust
4512 Pitt Street
Raleigh, NC 27609
Tel 919-733-6901

Holocaust: A Study of Genocide

Board of Education of the City of New York
Division of Curriculum and Instruction
100 Livingston Street
Brooklyn, NY 11201

The Holocaust: A Turning Point of Our Time

Author: Leon Stein
A five-day Holocaust and teacher's guide for secondary schools.

Holocaust Memorial Foundation of Illinois
4255 West Main Street
Skokie, IL 60076-2063
Tel 708-677-4640
Fax 708-677-4684

Holocaust: Can It Happen to Me?

State of Florida, Department of Education
Holocaust Documentation and Education Center, Inc.
Florida International University
NE 151 Street and Biscayne Boulevard
North Miami, FL 33161

The Holocaust and Genocide: A Search for Conscience

A curriculum guide and student anthology.

Anti-Defamation League of B'nai B'rith
823 United Nations Plaza
New York, NY 10017

The Holocaust: Prejudice Unleashed

Secondary school curriculum.

Ohio Council on Holocaust Education
Ohio Department of Education
65 Front Street, Room 1005
Columbus, OH 43266-0308

The Holocaust: The World and the Jews, 1933–1945

Author: Seymour Rossel
This book shows students how to examine photographs and to read official documents and eyewitness accounts to learn about the Holocaust; each chapter is followed by a review section and issues; useful resource for teachers of all levels.

Behrman House, Inc.
235 Watchung Avenue
West Orange, New Jersey 07052

Human Rights: The Struggle for Freedom, Dignity and Equality: Resource Guide

Connecticut State Department of Education
Bureau of Curriculum
Box 2219
Hartford, CT 06145

Life Unworthy of Life: A Holocaust Curriculum

Authors: Dr. Sidney M. Bolkosky, Betty Rothberg Ellias, Dr. David Harris

Glencoe Press
P.O. Box 543
Blacklick, Ohio 43004
Tel 800-334-7344

This curriculum is included in the U.S. Department of Education's National Diffusion Network; to arrange for in-service training, contact:

The Center for the Study of the Child
914 Lincoln Avenue
Ann Arbor, MI 48104-3525
Tel 313-761-6440
E-Mail PJNag@aol.com

Martyrdom and Resistance

Oldest and largest continuously circulating publication on the Holocaust.

48 West 37th Street
New York, NY 10018-7408

Model Curriculum for Human Rights and Genocide

California State Board of Education
Bureau of Publications Sales
P.O. Box 271
Sacramento, CA 95802-0271

The Nevada Study on the Holocaust Curriculum Guide

Nevada Governor's Advisory Council on Education Relating to the Holocaust
3909 S. Maryland Parkway, Suite 400
Las Vegas, NV 89118-7520

Tel 702-732-0556
Fax 702-732-3228

Pathways Through the Holocaust: An Oral History by Eyewitnesses

Author: Clara Isaacman, illustrations by Janet Katz
Information about the Holocaust and stories by survivors followed by questions and additional materials from the Jewish tradition; elementary and junior high/middle school levels.

KTAV Publishing House, Inc.
P.O. Box 6249
900 Jefferson Street
Hoboken, NJ 07030
Tel 201-963-9524

The Spirit That Moves Us

A literature-based resource guide for teaching about diversity, prejudice, human rights, and the Holocaust for kindergarten through grade four.

Holocaust Human Rights Center of Maine
RR 1, Box 825
Palermo, ME 04354
Tel 207-993-2620

The Record: The Holocaust in History, 1933–1945

Newspaper format prepared in conjunction with the National Council for Social Studies; discussion and study guide included.

Anti-Defamation League of B'nai B'rith
ADL Materials Library
22-D Hollywood Avenue
Ho-Ho-Kus, NJ 07423
Tel 800-343-5540

Remember Our Faces, Teaching About the Holocaust

ERIC Clearinghouse for Social Studies/Social Science Education
Bloomington, IN 47424

Resource Materials for Teaching About the Holocaust in United States History, Grade 11

Hartford County Public Schools
45 East Gordon Street
Bel Air, MD 21014

South Carolina Voices: Lessons from the Holocaust

Author: Linda Scher

South Carolina Department of Education
South Carolina Council on the Holocaust
1429 Senate Street, Room 801
Columbia, SC 29201
Tel 803-734-8385
Fax 803-734-8624

A Study of the Holocaust and Genocide

K–12 Curriculum
New Jersey Commission on Holocaust Education
225 West State Street, CN 500
Trenton, NJ 08625
Tel 609-767-5757

Teaching About the Holocaust and Genocide

State University of New York
The State Education Department
Bureau of Curriculum and Development
Albany, NY 12234

Teaching the Past Describes Today . . . Tomorrow . . . Human Rights Education—Focus: The Holocaust

Author: B.J. Brewer

State of Virginia
Social Studies Service
Division of Humanities and Secondary Administration
Virginia Department of Education
P.O. Box 6-Q
Richmond, VA 23216

The Virginia Children's Holocaust Essay Contest

P.O. Box 10865
Arlington, VA 22210
Tel 703-525-0842

Other Sources

Catalogs of resources and materials for teaching the Holocaust:

The Center for Learning
Shipping/Business Office
P.O. Box 910
Villa Maria, PA 16155
Tel 412-964-8083
    800-767-9090
Fax 412-964-8992
    or
Administrative/Editorial Office
21590 Center Ridge Road
Rocky River, Ohio 44116
Tel 216-331-1404
Fax 216-331-5414

Social Studies School Service
10200 Jefferson Boulevard, Room J211
P.O. Box 802
Culver City, CA 90232-0802
Tel 800-421-4246
    310-839-2436
Fax 310-839-2249

Collection of complete sets of teachers' guides and curricula for teaching the Holocaust from states, provinces, and cities:

Doris Rauch
Collections Development Dept.
Harriet Irving Library
University of New Brunswick
P.O. Box 7500
Fredericton, NB E3B 5H5
Canada
Tel 506-453-4760
Fax 506-453-4595
E-mail DORIS@UNB.CA

Directory of Holocaust organizations and their services:

Association of Holocaust Organizations
Holocaust Resource Center and Archives
Queensborough Community College
Bayside, NY 11364
Tel 718-225-0378
Fax 718-423-9620

Guides and materials from the U.S. Holocaust Memorial Museum:

Resource Center for Educators
Kristy L. Brosius, Resource Center Coordinator
100 Raoul Wallenberg Place, SW
Washington, DC 20024-2150
Tel 202-488-2661
Fax 202-488-6137
E-mail education@ushmm.org

The Resource Center for Educators has sample curriculum guides; bibliographies; journals; articles; files from states, countries, and organizations; and media resources. Available at no charge: *An Introductory Packet for Educators* that contains Guidelines for Teaching About the Holocaust, Annotated Bibliography, and Annotated Videography. Contact for information on the National Writing and Art Contest on the Holocaust.

Updated list of state requirements for Holocaust Education:

Dorene Randolph
U.S. Holocaust Memorial Museum
100 Raoul Wallenberg Place, SW
Washington, DC 20024
Tel 202-488-0400
Fax 202-488-2690

Information on Holocaust education materials

Reference Librarian
Simon Wiesenthal Center Library and Archives
9760 W. Pico Boulevard
Los Angeles, CA 90035-4792
Tel 310-553-9036, ext. 292
Fax 310-553-8659/310-277-5558
E-mail simonwie@class.org

Jewish community relations councils

JCRCs are liaisons between the local Jewish community federations and the community at large. Many can assist educators in contacting Holocaust survivors and obtaining other educational information. A list of Jewish federations is in the *American Jewish Yearbook*, published by the American Jewish Committee.

American Jewish Committee
165 East 56th Street

New York, NY 10022
Tel 212-751-4000

Media Resources

Films/Videos

Several of these films are also available for rental in video stores and public libraries.

About the Holocaust (JM, S)

> Young American woman, daughter of a survivor, describes her quest to learn about the Holocaust and why studying it is important now; produced by the Holocaust Survivors Film Project and includes documentary footage as well as firsthand survivor accounts.

> ADL Materials Library
> 22-D Hollywood Avenue
> Ho-Ho-Kus, NJ 07423
> Tel 800-343-5540

Alan and Naomi (JM, E)

> Story of Jewish boy in Brooklyn who befriends a troubled French refugee; based on the novel of the same title.

> Facets Video
> 1517 West Fullerton Avenue
> Chicago, IL 60614
> Tel 800-331-6197

Camera of My Family: Four Generations in Germany, 1845–1945 (JM, S)

> Award-winning story of an upper-middle class German-Jewish family; illustrates fate of all European Jews during Holocaust.

> ADL Materials Library
> 22-D Hollywood Avenue
> Ho-Ho-Kus, NJ 07423
> Tel 800-343-5540

The Courage to Care (JM, S)

> Documentary about ordinary people who helped Holocaust victims; nominated for an Academy Award in 1986.

Other Sources   177

Zenger Video
10200 Jefferson Boulevard, Room 902
P.O. Box 802
Culver City, CA 90232-0802
Tel 800-421-4246

Daniel's Story(E, JM)

Uses archival photographs and film footage to describe the Holocaust from the perspective of a Jewish child growing up in Nazi Germany; no images of graphic horror; resource packet available. Contact Kristy Brosius, Resource Center Coordinator at the museum, for a list of resource centers that loan copies of this video.

United States Holocaust Memorial Museum
100 Raoul Wallenberg Place, SW
Washington, DC 20024-2150
Tel 202-488-0400

The Diary of Anne Frank (JM, S)

Award-winning adaptation of the book.

Facets Video
1517 West Fullerton Avenue
Chicago, IL 60614
Tel 800-331-6197

Dear Kitty (JM, S)

Life of Anne Frank and historical background on the Holocaust.

Anne Frank Center
106 East 19th Street
New York, NY 10003
Tel 212-529-9532

Flames in the Ashes (S)

Historic film footage of the ways the Jews resisted the Nazis; English subtitles.

Ergo Media, Inc.
P.O. Box 2037
Teaneck, NJ 07666
Tel 800-695-3746

Genocide, 1941–1945 (JM, S)

Archival film footage and testimonies provide overview of the destruction of the European Jews.

Arts and Entertainment
Tel 800-423-1212

A&E Home Video
P.O. Box 2284
South Burlington, VT 05407

The Hangman (JM, S)

Animation illustrates Maurice Ogden's poem; illustrates role of individual responsibility and the bystander in the Holocaust.

CRM
2215 Faraday, Suite F
Carlsbad, CA 92008
Tel 800-421-0833

Holocaust: Liberation of Auschwitz (S)

Graphic film footage of the liberation of Auschwitz and commentary on daily life by Soviet cameraman.

Zenger Videos
10200 Jefferson Boulevard, Room 902
P.O. Box 802
Culver City, CA 90232-0802
Tel 800-421-4246

The Holocaust: Through Our Own Eyes (JM, S)

Survivor testimonies supplemented with archival photographs and film footage; some graphic material; resource packet available.

Midwest Center for Holocaust Education
5801 West 115th Street, Suite 106
Overland Park, KS 66211
Tel 913-491-9665
Fax 913-491-9742

Image Before My Eyes (JM, S)

Documentary recreates Jewish life in Poland prior to Holocaust.

Simon Wiesenthal Center
Yeshiva University of Los Angeles

9760 W. Pico Boulevard
Los Angeles, CA 90035
Tel 310-553-9036

Korczak (JM, S)

Based on true story of Janusz Korczak, the Polish doctor who cared for orphans in the Warsaw Ghetto and then perished with them in Treblinka.

New York Films Video
16 W. 61st Street
New York, NY 10023
Tel 212-247-6110

The Last Chapter (JM, S)

History of Jews in Poland from earliest communities through postwar period.

J.C. Entertainment
450 7th Avenue, Suite 2702
New York, NY 10123
Tel 212-967-3904

The Last Sea (S)

Uses historic film footage to tell of postwar Jewish exodus from Europe to Israel.

Ergo Media, Inc.
P.O. Box 2037
Teaneck, NJ 07666
Tel 800-695-3746

The Last Seven Months of Anne Frank (JM, S)

Documentary of people who were with Anne Frank and her family during the final months of her life.

Simon Wiesenthal Center
Media Department
9760 W. Pico Boulevard,
Los Angeles, CA 90035
Tel 213-553-9036, ext. 237

The Life of Adolf Hitler (JM, S)

Chronological account of major events from the rise of Nazism to end of World War II using archival film footage.

Video Yesterday
Box C
Sandy Hook, CT 06482
Tel 800-243-0987

Lodz Ghetto (JM, S)

Documentary using photographs, slides, film footage, and written accounts by Jews in the Lodz Ghetto in Poland; teacher's guide available from Anti-Defamation League.

Jewish Heritage Project, Inc.
150 Franklin Street, #1W
New York, NY 10003
Tel 212-925-9067

Man Alive: Journey to Prague: A Remembrance (JM, S)

Narrative of a Holocaust survivor who returns to Prague, Czechoslovakia, and recalls life growing up in the Jewish community.

Films Incorporated
5547 N. Ravenswood
Chicago, IL 60640-1199
Tel 312-878-2600

More Than Broken Glass: Memories of Kristallnacht (S)

Describes Jewish life in Germany prior to and during the Holocaust using survivor interviews, archival film footage, and photographs.

Ergo Media, Inc.
P.O. Box 2037
Teaneck, NJ 07666
Tel 800-695-3746

Murderers Among Us: The Simon Wiesenthal Story (S)

True story of the Holocaust survivor who dedicated himself to bringing Nazis to justice.

Zenger Videos
10200 Jefferson Boulevard, Room 902
P.O. Box 802
Culver City, CA 90232-0802
Tel 800-421-4246

Night and Fog (S)

Documentary contrasts contemporary film footage with historic footage shot inside concentration camps; award-winning; some graphic footage; English subtitles.

Video Yesterday
Box C
Sandy Hook, CT 06482
Tel 800-243-0987

Obedience (JM, S)

Shows the experiment conducted at Yale University to test the willingness of people to follow orders even though they inflict pain on others.

Penn State Audio-Visuals Service
Tel 800-826-0132

Opening the Gates of Hell (S)

Interviews, photographs, and film footage of camps that were liberated by the Americans; some graphic scenes.

Ergo Media, Inc.
P.O. Box 2037
Teaneck, NJ 07666
Tel 800-695-3746

The Other Side of Faith (JM, S)

First-person narrative of Polish Catholic teenager who hid Jews in her home for two and a half years.

Film and Video Foundation
1800 K Street, NW, Suite 1120
Washington, DC 20006
Tel 202-429-9320

Persecuted and Forgotten (S)

Interviews and personal accounts of Gypsies who were persecuted during the Holocaust and the continuing discrimination against them.

EBS Productions
330 Ritch Street
San Francisco, CA 94107
Tel 415-495-2327

Raoul Wallenberg: Between the Lines (S)

Story of the Swedish diplomat's efforts to save Hungarian Jews.

Social Studies School Services
10200 Jefferson Boulevard, Room J
P.O. Box 802
Culver, City, CA 90232-0802
Tel 800-421-4246

Riga: A Tale of Two Ghettos (JM, S)

Story of Riga Ghetto using survivor testimony, drawings, and photos.

U.S. Holocaust Memorial Museum
100 Raoul Wallenberg Place, SW
Washington, DC 20024-2150
Tel 202-488-0400

Ripples in Time (JM, S)

Survivor experiences including concentration camps and in hiding.

North Carolina Council on the Holocaust
2330 Lash Avenue
Raleigh, NC 27606
Tel 919-787-9232

Schindler's List (S)

Story of a German business profiteer who tries to save Jewish workers in his Polish factories. Secondary school educators can contact The Gold Group (Tel 800-574-5754) to find out if their state is participating in the program to make the film available to schools. For information on how to obtain a "Viewers Guide," edited by Dr. Alex Grobman, Director of Martyrs Memorial and Museum of the Holocaust, contact museum personnel at 6505 Wilshire Boulevard, Los Angeles, CA 90048 (Tel 213-852-3242).

SWANK Motion Pictures Distributors
Tel 800-876-5577

Shoah (JM, S)

Nine-and-a-half-hour film provides an oral history of the Holocaust; intersperses contemporary footage of camps, towns, and railways with interviews with victims, perpetrators, and bystanders; book with same title contains complete text of film.

Simon Wiesenthal Center
Yeshiva University of Los Angeles
9760 W. Pico Boulevard
Los Angeles, CA 90035
Tel 310-553-9036

Susan (JM, S)

The youngest survivor of Dr. Mengele's medical experiments in Auschwitz tells her personal story.

KSU Teleproductions
Kent State University
C-105, Music and Speech Building
Kent, OH 44242
Tel 216-672-2810

Triumph of Memory (JM, S)

Non-Jewish resistance fighters describe the camps and their horrors; also includes information about the Gypsies.

PBS Videos
1320 Braddock Place
Alexandria, VA 22314-1698
Tel 800-344-3337

Triumph of the Will (JM, S)

Propaganda film of the 1943 Nuremberg Nazi party rally.

Zenger Videos
10200 Jefferson Boulevard, Room 902
P.O. Box 802
Culver City, CA 90232-0802
Tel 800-421-4246

The Wannsee Conference (S)

Dramatization of the conference where Nazis leaders discussed the implementation of the Final Solution. English subtitles.

Zenger Videos
10200 Jefferson Boulevard, Room 902
P.O. Box 802
Culver City, CA 90232-0802
Tel 800-421-4246

The Warsaw Ghetto (JM, S)

Documentary using historic film footage and narrated by a ghetto survivor

Zenger Video
10200 Jefferson Blvd., Room 902
P.O. Box 802
Culver City, CA 90232-0802
Tel 800-421-4246

The Wave (S)

Based on true experiences in a high-school classroom where the teacher demonstrates with the students the conditions leading to Nazism. Book of same title available.

Films Incorporated
5547 N. Ravenswood Avenue
Chicago, IL 60640
Tel 312-878-2600

Weapons of the Spirit (JM, S)

Story of small French Protestant village that hid 5,000 Jews, many of them children, from the Nazis.

Zenger Video
10200 Jefferson Boulevard, Room 902
P.O. Box 802
Culver City, CA 90232-0802
Tel 800-421-4246

Witness to the Holocaust (JM, S)

Series of seven documentaries using photographs, historic film footage, and survivor narration; topics cover the full range of the Holocaust from the rise of Nazism to Liberation.

ADL Materials Library
22-D Hollywood Avenue
Ho-Ho-Kus, NJ 07423
Tel 800-343-5540

World War II: The Propaganda Battle (JM, S)

Examines how propaganda and mass media were used to manipulate public opinion.

PBS Videos
1320 Braddock Place
Alexandria, VA 22314-1698
Tel 800-344-3337

Additional Titles of Films/Videos

The following titles also may be of interest. Contact your local school media center, public library, or video store for more information.

The Attic: The Hiding of Anne Frank

Au Revoir Les Enfants (Goodbye, Children)

The Boat Is Full

Children of Terezin

Judgment at Nuremberg

Kitty: Return to Auschwitz

The Legacy of Anne Frank

Lena: My 100 Children

Let My People Go

Miracle at Moreau

Music of Auschwitz

Robert Clary, A5714: A Memoir of Liberation

Thunder in Munich

Audio Recordings

For information about the following audio recordings, contact your school resource center or public library.

Abba Kovner—My Little Sister and Other Poems

Anne Frank: The Dairy of a Young Girl

Children of the Holocaust, The Lost Generation

Dan Pagis—Transformation

Hitler on the Air

I Never Saw Another Butterfly

Music from the Paradise Ghetto

Night

Paris: Natives and Newcomers

Songs of the Ghettos

Warsaw: From Tradition to Modernity

We Who Survive

Index of Authors

The index of authors lists only the page numbers of the primary description of their works.

Index of Book Titles by Chapter and Genre

This index lists only the page number of the primary description of a work.

3 ▪ They Were There: Personal Narratives, Biographies, Autobiographies, Poetry

4 ▪ We Learn from Stories: Historical Fiction

5 • We Recreate Through Drama: Plays

6 • It Must Not Happen Again: Fiction, Nonfiction